Business Agility

Business Agility

Sustainable Prosperity in a Relentlessly Competitive World

Michael Hugos

WILEY

John Wiley & Sons, Inc.

Published by John Wiley & Sons, Inc., Hoboken, New Jersey.
Published simultaneously in Canada.

For general information on our other products and services, or technical support, please contact our Customer Care Department within the United States at 800-762-2974, outside the United States at 317-572-3993 or fax 317-572-4002.

Wiley also publishes its books in a variety of electronic formats. Some content that appears in print may not be available in electronic books.

For more information about Wiley products, visit our Web site at http://www.wiley.com.

Library of Congress Cataloging-in-Publication Data

Hugos, Michael H.
    Business agility : sustainable prosperity in a relentlessly competitive
world / Michael Hugos.
        p. cm. – (Microsoft executive leadership series)
    Includes bibliographical references and index.
    ISBN 978-0-470-41345-6 (cloth)
    1. Entrepreneurship.   2. Competition, International.   3. Globalization.
4. Organizational change.   5. Technological innovations.   I. Title.
    HB615.H85 2009
    658.4′062–dc22

                                                            2008042934

Printed in the United States of America.

10   9   8   7   6   5   4   3   2   1

To my wife Venetia

Contents

Microsoft Executive Leadership Series: Series Foreword

The Microsoft Executive Leadership Series provides leaders with inspiration and examples to consider when forming business strategies to stand the test of time. As the pace of change quickens and the influence of social demographics, the impact of educational reform, and the impetus of national interests evolve, organizations that understand and embrace these underlying forces can build strategy on solid ground. Increasingly, information technology is bridging social, educational, and international distances and empowering people to perform at their fullest potential. Organizations that succeed in the enlightened use of technology will increasingly differentiate themselves in the marketplace for talent, raw materials, and customers.

I talk nearly every day to executives and policy makers grappling with issues like globalization, workforce evolution, and the impact of technology on people and processes. The idea for this series came from those conversations—we see it as a way to distill what we've learned as a company into actionable intelligence. The authors bring independent perspectives, expertise, and experience. We hope their insights will spark dialogues within organizations, among communities, and between partners about the critical relationship between people and technology in the workplace of the future.

I hope you enjoy this title in the Microsoft Executive Leadership Series and find it useful as you plan for the expected and unexpected developments ahead for your organization. It's our privilege and our commitment to be part of that conversation.

DANIEL W. RASMUS
General Editor, Microsoft Executive Leadership Series

Titles in the Executive Leadership Series:

Rules to Break and Laws to Follow by Don Peppers & Martha Rogers, 2008.

Generation Blend by Rob Salkowitz, 2008.

Uniting the Virtual Workforce by Karen Sobel Lojeski & Richard Reilly, 2008.

Drive Business Performance by Bruno Aziza & Joey Fitts, 2008.

Listening to the Future by Daniel W. Rasmus with Rob Salkowitz, 2008.

Business Agility by Michael Hugos, 2009.

Generation X-ecutive by Rob Salkowitz, 2009.

Leading the Virtual Workforce by Karen Sobel Lojeski & Richard Reilly, 2009.

The implications of our global real time economy affect us all. Its rise has been much discussed for the last 30 years or so, and during that time this economy evolved in ways that were often slow and subtle. Sometimes it even seemed like the real time economy was more about words than reality. Now we know otherwise. The global economy has a life of its own; it lives in real time; and we are all a part of it. Hello, brave new world.

The technical and economic infrastructure that makes this economy possible has gone from something of academic interest and speculation to something that now sets the daily tempo and working conditions of our lives. This economy is at times a pretty harsh taskmaster. We wonder if there is a way to get back some of the personal control over our careers and our lifestyles that seems to have disappeared.

Our world is driven by the convergence of a host of forces that are transforming the way we live. There is relentless economic competition, outsourcing of white-collar jobs and manufacturing jobs to lower-wage countries, rising prices for basic commodities like food and fuel, and the climate change effects resulting from the actions of all of us.

Our challenge is clear enough. It is to learn to use this economy and the information and communications technologies that enable it to operate so as to achieve and sustain a good life, one that responds to our basic needs for sustenance and also responds to our higher needs for belonging, esteem, and self-actualization. In rising to this challenge, many things will change.

We are sailors on an ocean of change and the organizations we are part of are the ships we sail. We cannot sail against the prevailing winds, but we can learn to work with the wind and the waves and harness their energy to arrive at the destinations we aspire to reach. It is in this process of learning that some of our greatest opportunities lie.

The first two chapters of this book define the business challenges we must confront and also some of the new opportunities and technologies available to us to use in addressing these challenges. Chapters 3 and 4 outline operating principles and strategies we can use to respond to these challenges. Each chapter provides case studies and examples to illustrate the ideas presented.

The next two chapters are focused on illustrating different aspects of the operating model of businesses built to thrive in the real-time global economy—what this book calls responsive. Chapter 5 goes into further detail on how such organizations work, and Chapter 6 presents examples and discusses ways to make best use of technology to empower the people and operations of these organizations.

The last two chapters address two themes that are central to making the responsive organization happen. The first theme is desire, and the second theme is innovation. Chapter 7 examines barriers that test our desire and our collective will to create responsive organizations, and it presents techniques for surmounting these obstacles. Chapter 8 provides insights into the process so important for creating something new: innovation. The responsive organization comes partly from new ideas and partly from old ideas combined in new ways. This chapter presents those ideas in the form of five key characteristics that describe what a responsive organization is and how it operates.

My intention in writing this book is to articulate a handful of powerful trends that are shaping our businesses and our lives in this century and to offer a handful of simple yet equally powerful principles and techniques for responding to these trends. We live in interesting times. We live in the best of times. I am always glad to hear your comments, your questions, or your further insights on the subjects discussed here.

Please feel free to contact me via my website: www.michaelhugos .com, or at my blog "Business Agility & Sustainable Prosperity." My email address is: mhugos@yahoo.com.

MICHAEL HUGOS
Chicago, IL
December 2008

CHAPTER 1

Responsiveness Trumps Efficiency

Today's global economy squeezes profit margins more efficiently than ever before. Electronically connected global markets are doing what markets do so well; the commodities traders and stockbrokers call it "efficient price discovery." That phrase means global markets are constantly finding the lowest price for all basic commodities and services based on current supply and demand—everything from blue jeans to fuel oil, and hotel rooms to accounting services—and constantly resetting those prices as conditions change.

This market driven efficient price discovery tends to relentlessly reduce profits and drives the prices people can charge for products and services closer and closer to their cost of production (sometimes even below their cost of production). Companies are always moving their production to low-cost labor markets and outsourcing activities in a scramble to lower the cost of production so that they can still make a profit at price points set by the market.

For this reason, the best profits for most companies no longer come from standard or commodity products; the best profits are now to be found in new and creative products and services. If these new products catch on, for a while they have no competition and there is lots of demand so prices stay high. But products and services are new and innovative for only a short time. Then they become commodities because they get copied and offered at lower prices. And when that happens, profit margins drop again.

Most profitable opportunities in the global economy are, by definition, short-term opportunities. Companies need to respond and act quickly in order to capitalize on opportunities that arise. This has always been true, but now it is critical if a company is going to maintain its long-term profitability.

THE WORLD BEHAVES LIKE A STOCK MARKET

The Internet and the search engines and the trading and procurement systems that make global markets possible also do something else. They provide massive and continuous flows of data the likes of which we used to see only in connection with financial markets, such as stock and futures markets. Now our economy everywhere is generating similar flows of data. Companies generate data flows from their internal systems; e-commerce and supply chain networks generate more data flows that go between companies; and the Internet moves all this data from anywhere to anywhere 24 hours a day, seven days a week.

These real-time data flows cause the whole world to behave like a giant stock market with all the volatility and uncertainty that goes along with such markets. And because real-time data is available, we are all doing business in real time now whether we know it or not. Just as stockbrokers use real time stock market data to constantly monitor and react to their markets, so too can people in business use available real-time data to monitor their own markets and react quickly as situations change.

The very fact that more and more companies are connecting up with e-commerce and electronic trading networks means that the markets they work in are becoming more volatile. Because information is available in real time, people are learning to react more quickly. Change ripples through markets much faster than ever was possible in the industrial economy. Supply and demand data for products and services are communicated quickly so the prices of those products change quickly (just like stock prices). Gone are the days when people could confidently predict the price of any commodity for more than a month or two.

Companies that succeed are learning to make continuous small adjustments in their operations to respond as conditions change, and they are learning to continuously enhance their products and services with new features as their customers' desires evolve. They learn to make money from many small adjustments and from some occasional big wins—just as stock traders do.

Companies must attain and maintain a level of "good-enough" efficiency, but unless a company is the low-cost leader in its market, it cannot use efficiency alone to generate profits. For the most part, it is now customer responsiveness that generates profits in the form of customers paying slightly higher prices for products and services that they find more responsive to their needs. Since these products deliver more value, people are willing to pay more.

Opportunities to make money by being responsive have exploded. There are far more ways to use responsiveness to attract customers than there are ways to use efficiency and low prices. This is because there are so many different kinds of customers, and each is looking for slightly different mixes of products and services. Constantly changing environments and customer needs enable responsive companies to offer continuously evolving mixes of new products and services.

Companies respond to evolving needs and desires of specific groups of customers by wrapping their products and services in tailored blankets of value-added services. Occasionally they find opportunities to introduce entirely new products and services. As profits on old products decline, profits are always to be found by creating new products that respond to new needs.

Responsiveness enables a company to consistently earn an additional gross margin of 2 to 4 percent (and sometimes more) than what it

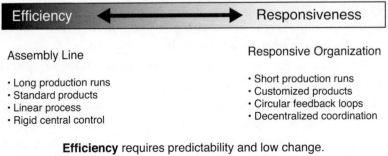

Efficiency requires predictability and low change.
Responsiveness to continuous change now creates more value.

FIGURE 1.1   Companies Exist on a Continuum between Two Needs

would otherwise earn for its commodity product or service alone.[1] This responsive focus on customer and market specialization is now the most promising and the most sustainable source of profits in our fluid, real-time economy. These ideas are summarized in Figure 1.1.

In this high-change global economy, *responsiveness trumps efficiency.*

EFFICIENCY IS ONLY HALF OF THE EQUATION

For the last few hundred years, the most important consideration in business was efficiency: producing products at the lowest possible cost. But now we are all part of a global labor force, and there are countries in Europe and North America that can no longer compete on efficiency alone because their labor costs (also known as people's salaries) are so high compared to labor costs in countries in Asia, Africa, and South America.

What is to be done? Will the economic boom for some countries be economic doom for others? That might be the case if the only economic force we considered is efficiency. But we are missing something important when we do this; in addition to efficiency, there is another economic force called responsiveness. Efficiency provides us with basic products and services at the lowest price. Responsiveness wraps those products and services in a blanket of value-added services that customize them to our particular needs and, in doing so, makes them more valuable to each of us.

Everybody has needs that go beyond efficiency. As soon as people are able to acquire the basics, they want something more (see Maslow's Hierarchy of Needs[2] as presented in his classic article "A Theory of Human Motivation"). A basic pair of sneakers costs about $20, but there are a whole lot of people willing to pay $100 or more for sneakers that respond to their other needs. A basic new car costs about $16,000 (or less), but there are many millions of people willing to pay much more to get cars that respond to their other needs.

People want what they want. They want a good price, but that doesn't mean they want the lowest price. People usually also want a tailored bundle of additional services and features wrapped around the basic product. They will pay extra for these other features as long as they meet expectations. Maslow's Hierarchy of Needs in Figure 1.2 shows that once a lower-level, basic need is filled, people aspire to filling higher-level needs.

Even the most basic commodity product can be wrapped in a blanket of value-added services that increases its value to particular customers because those value-added services provide features customers want. For instance, we have all seen how a commodity product like the coffee bean can be wrapped with a blanket of value-added services and so give rise to a whole industry. People will pay more for a good cup of coffee made just so and served in a cozy setting. And if the quality of the coffee and

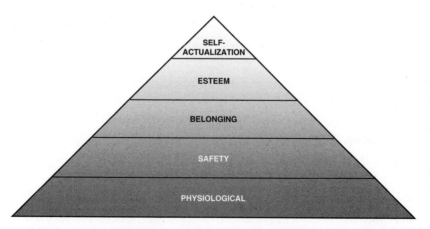

FIGURE 1.2   Maslow's Hierarchy of Needs

the coziness of the setting start to decline at one company, customers simply go elsewhere. People will pay more for a good product but they do not pay extra if they are not getting what they want.

Good customers (and most customers are good customers when you figure out what they really want) will pay a few percentage points more in order to get a carefully tailored bundle of goods and services from you that either solves an important problem of theirs or enables them to enjoy a major benefit. Who are the good customers in your business? How will you get more of them? What are the tailored solutions you offer them? How will you evolve these solutions over time to keep up with good customers' changing needs?

And here is another thing to think about: If you don't have many good customers, how will you keep your bad customers from destroying your profits and your business? Is efficiency alone a sufficient answer to this question?

TRADITIONAL BUSINESS MODELS ARE COMING UP SHORT

Many large, established companies are demonstrating that their traditional focus on efficiency no longer shields them from market fluctuations, nor does it deliver the profits it once did. Their business models need to be redesigned. They follow business strategies based on twentieth-century industrial concepts of efficiency, such as spreading fixed costs across huge numbers of units sold, scheduling long production runs, and assuming there is a steady, predictable demand for their products.

In reality, things such as stability and predictability are conspicuously absent from our global economy. Yet companies continue their old industrial strategies and continue to struggle with rigid multiyear plans and projects as they drift farther and farther away from alignment with constantly changing market conditions.

Then, when the alignment between company operations and actual customer demand becomes seriously out of balance, when finances drift deep into the red zone, companies have no other options for responding except to make sudden and drastic cuts in their operating expenses. They sell off businesses, close down factories, and disband whole groups. They lay off thousands of employees at a time.

These bouts of corporate cutting and restructuring happen with regularity now; they happen in good economies and bad economies. And individual companies go through these restructurings not just once but repeatedly. Why is this necessary? It would seem that something about the business models these companies follow, something about the way they are managed, must be seriously out of line with current realities.

The relentless focus on efficiency is the legacy of a frame of mind inherent in the culture of the industrial economy and its great invention: the assembly line. That mind-set attempts to organize every activity down to the lowest levels of detail. It makes rules and regulations for everything and then tries to run each activity over and over, faster and faster without changing anything. This is how you get economies of scale: greater and greater productivity at lower and lower costs. This is what we call efficiency. But this model is breaking down.

The assembly line requires things to stay the same long enough to churn out large quantities of predefined products and services. It is the best way to deliver masses of standard products and services at the lowest cost. But what happens when people no longer want standard products and services? What happens when product life cycles are measured in months instead of years? That lack of predictability throws a major wrench into the gears of the industrial efficiency model.

Business strategies that emphasize efficiency and economies of scale no longer yield the profits we seek because they are so vulnerable to unexpected and sudden changes. The efficiency model does not allow for much responsiveness since it concentrates on removing all extra capacity and reducing operating expenses to the absolute minimum.

EFFICIENCY WITHOUT RESPONSIVENESS WILL KILL YOUR COMPANY

Responsiveness calls for flexibility, and flexibility calls for maintaining some extra capacity and for budgeting additional money to be available when needs and opportunities arise. A single-minded focus on efficiency views this extra capacity and funding as wasteful and strives to remove it. So in the name of efficiency, companies give up the flexibility and responsiveness they need to handle unexpected situations.

The fast pace of events now overwhelms the assembly-line operating model and the efficiency mind-set that goes along with it. Companies spend years organizing work, writing out rules and procedures, and putting systems and facilities in place. Then the world changes in unpredictable and uncontrollable ways, and their plans don't work out because they become irrelevant so quickly.

I once worked for a chief executive officer (CEO) who was forever attempting to screw down operations as tight as a drum—cut staff and squeeze out the last ounce of cost in the name of ultimate efficiency. He would look at me with a maniacal gleam in his eyes and laugh as he chopped away at headcounts and budgets. His plan was always the same: In every situation, it was to cut costs and run operations hard and fast, day and night, and thus reap the profits of ultimate efficiency. That is the assembly-line mind-set.

The problem was that in spite of his best-laid plans, the world would change in unforeseen ways, and then he had no reserve and no flex in his operations with which to respond. So instead, he would pound the boardroom table at our monthly management meetings and insist there was no change; and if there was, well then everyone should just work harder (but we were already working at full capacity; he had seen to that).

The more he cut budgets and focused on efficiency, the less able we were to respond to customers' changing needs. We missed profitable opportunities to grow the business, and some of our biggest customers came to believe we were no longer capable of keeping up with their evolving business needs. They became dissatisfied with our service and began looking elsewhere for more responsive business partners.

CUSTOMER RELATIONSHIPS ARE THE MOST VALUABLE ASSET

That CEO forgot that the customer is the ultimate asset these days, not buildings or equipment or products. Those things can readily be acquired from many different sources, but by far the hardest thing to acquire is customers. The opportunity in business now is to apply what you know about your customers and what you know about your products to create a tailored bundle of products and value-added services that constantly evolves to best fit their needs.

As you combine your knowledge of your customers and your knowledge of the products you sell, you become, in effect, your customers' purchasing agent. You're someone constantly seeking the best mix of your products and services to fit your customers' changing situations. You are no longer just a clever gadfly trying to sell them something they don't really need. Your fate is now much more tied up with that of your customers. If they don't grow and prosper, you won't either.

Think of your customers as your capital and think of responsiveness as the way to earn interest on that capital. The bigger your base of customers, the more the opportunities there are to be responsive to their changing needs (and earn a higher rate of interest). Opportunities these days quickly evolve into other opportunities; one opportunity usually leads to another. Learn to ride the waves of change. Develop a reputation for responsiveness; your customers will seek you out for that very reason.

THE VALUE-ADDED PAPER CUP

Let me provide an example of tailoring products and services to respond to customer needs. For six years I was the chief information officer of a national distributor of food-service disposables and janitorial supplies for restaurant chains, healthcare facilities, and grocery stores (network services) company. We're talking paper cups, plastic forks, paper towels, and floor wax. These are humble products, and a paper cup is a commodity product if there ever was one. What do you suppose is the profit margin on a paper cup? The answer is "not much," and it gets lower all the time.[3]

So our challenge was to make our products more valuable and earn a higher profit. I led a project team from the company's sales, customer service, information technology, and finance organizations, and we devised a menu of about 50 different value-added services that salespeople could then mix and match to meet specific customer needs.

We made it very easy and convenient for customers to find and order our cups by providing an online product catalog that let them search on many different product parameters (size, strength, color, materials used, etc.). We also set up the product catalog to remind them to order other items that normally go along with cups, such as lids and sleeves.

We let customers place and track their orders online so they could know when their supplies would be delivered. We also created customized labels and packing boxes so that when cups were delivered, customers could quickly receive, store, and retrieve them.

We enhanced our billing system to streamline the processing of invoices by customers and reduce their costs of doing business with us. We sent invoices in whatever format customers wanted so they could automatically import them into their accounts payable systems. We even preprocessed invoices, inserting customers' general ledger codes into every line item on invoices so those costs could be automatically disbursed to their general ledger systems.

Finally, we provided customers with easy-to-use Web-based reporting that let them see how many cups (and other products too) they ordered at each of their ordering locations over any period of time, from one day to two years. They could monitor their spending and get detailed data for planning and budgeting, along with real-time insight into usage patterns and purchasing trends (see Figure 1.3).

We negotiated a set of service-level agreements (SLAs) with customers and then used a simple business process management (BPM) system and some Web-based dashboards to track our actual performance against customer SLAs. The business process management system compared customer purchase orders with our advance ship notices and invoices to automatically calculate the performance statistics displayed on the dashboards (things like order fill rates, on-time delivery rate, and perfect order rates). These dashboards were updated every 24 hours and could be accessed on our Web site by customers as well as our own people.

We also experimented with customer contracts where, if we met or exceeded our SLA targets in one quarter, we had the right to raise our prices by a fraction of a percent in the following quarter. This was a way

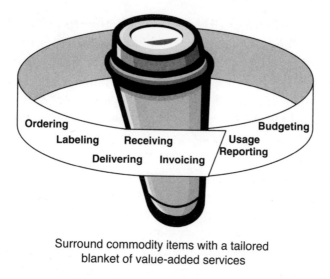

Surround commodity items with a tailored
blanket of value-added services

FIGURE 1.3 The Value-Added Paper Cup

for customers to share a bit of the extra value we delivered to them by
our high service levels.

In short, we turned our products into tailored solutions that solved
important problems for our customers. And therefore, we could sell our
paper cups for a few percentage points more than our competitors. We
did so by making strategic investments in information technology (IT).
This is an example of employing IT as a profit center instead of as a cost
center. This is what the future looks like.

Every company has its equivalent of the paper cup. Figure out how
your company can take its otherwise commodity products and tailor
them to respond to your customers' changing needs. Once you start this
process, it can take on a life of its own; your company will find itself
engaged in a process of continuous response to change and that process
can transform your business.

A MOST AMAZING INNOVATION

The most profound innovation since the assembly line is staring us
right in the face. But we don't see it because we are so busy looking for

something else. For most of us, the word "innovation" still conjures up images of new gadgets, such as technology to turn water into gasoline, black boxes to project moving 3-D holograms from our TV sets, and biotech breakthroughs that reverse the aging process.

Of course, some of these things will come to pass. But in our fixation on individual gadgets, we are missing an innovation that is based more on process than it is on technology. Consider this: A hundred years ago there was a process-based innovation in business so profound it became the basis for the economy of the industrial age. That process was the assembly line. The assembly line delivered a new level of efficiency that became the basis for prosperity in the industrial economy.

Another process-based innovation is once again sprouting in our midst. It is a business operating model coming to be known variously as the agile enterprise or real-time enterprise or responsive organization.[4] Companies using this operating model are delivering customer value and operating profits that will become the basis for prosperity in the real-time global economy. The responsive organization is a human-driven organization whose primary assets are the relationships that exist between its employees and its customers and suppliers. It is capable of endless adaptations and reconfigurations; it evolves as its customers evolve. It is enabled by the technology it uses but is not controlled or dominated by its technology.

With markets constantly moving and product life cycles often measured in months, companies can no longer hope to fine-tune their operations to fit some existing set of conditions and then expect simply to run those operations unchanged for years and years. That was the old industrial model; we need something more responsive now—something that constantly adjusts to changes and opportunities.

A responsive organization constantly makes many small adjustments to better respond to its changing environment. In doing so it reduces costs and increases revenues every day. No one adjustment by itself may be all that significant, but the cumulative effect of all of them over time is enormous—just like the effect of compound interest over time.

Traditional organizations are now caught in an inexorable squeeze as profit margins on their commodity products and services are relentlessly ratcheted down by the global economy. The agile enterprise is an enterprise that has learned how to make profits from many small adjustments and some occasional big wins. Soon enough those companies that cannot earn profits from constant small adjustments (and a few big wins) will hardly be profitable at all.

Just as we recognize the efficiency of the assembly line as the great wealth producer of the industrial economy, we will see the responsiveness of the real-time enterprise as the great wealth producer of the information economy.

USING INFORMATION TECHNOLOGY TO MAKE MONEY

We need to change our thinking about what information technology contributes to an organization. In the industrial economy of the last century, we were used to viewing computing as a back-office function—a cost center. The reality now is that IT is part of the production capacity of a company; if used well, it is a profit center. We need to ask ourselves what we can do with IT that our customers will pay us for; what value-added services can we provide them; and how can we use IT to deliver those services?

Most business responsiveness comes from customizing existing products and services with a mix of value-added services, and most value-added services are information based. That's because they must be customized to meet particular needs of particular customers. What is valuable to one customer in one situation is not valuable to another customer in a different situation.

Opportunities to make money by being responsive have exploded. Constantly changing environments and customer needs enable responsive companies to offer continuously evolving mixes of products and services. As profits on old products decline, profits are always to be found by creating new products that respond to new needs.

Get to know your company's customers; go on sales calls; take note of how your customers talk about your products and the questions they ask. Concentrate on what customers like and don't like about your products.

Find out what your competitors are doing. How do their products' features and prices compare with yours? Think about what will make the products your company sells more attractive. How can IT improve the things customers like and reduce those that they don't like?

ALL PRODUCTS AND SERVICES HAVE TWO COMPONENTS

As you ponder these questions, remember that all products have two components. The first component is the basic product or service itself; the price for that is set by the market, not by individual companies. And products quickly become commodities because your competitors have or soon develop similar products, so the prices you can charge get ratcheted down.

The second component is made up of the information about your product and the value-added services that surround it. This is what enables customers to find and evaluate your product, to understand how to use it, and to get the results and benefits they want from it (see Figure 1.4).

This second component is where above-market prices and profits are to be found. Through creative use of the information component, you can wrap any commodity product with a mix of value-added services that make it more useful and for which customers will pay a little extra. Information technology lowers the cost and expands capacity to deliver

Actual item or service by itself is often just a commodity; easily copied and offered by others; very low profit margins

Information component guides customer in selection and use of product; tailored to each customer so each achieves its desired results and benefits; generates best profit margins

FIGURE 1.4 Two Components Make Up Every Product

the information component. This is where skillful use of IT enables a company to earn higher profits.

Figure out how to leverage information about the products your company sells and information about whom it sells these products to. Figure out how to use IT to deliver a mix of value-added services tailored to your customers' changing needs so that you deliver more value to customers, and you will see your IT organization become a profit center.

And your company can take that straight to the bottom line.

NOTES

1. From 1990 to 1994 at global electronics distributor Anixter International (www. anixter.com) and from 2000 to 2005 at foodservice and janitorial products distributor Network Services Company (www.nsconline.com) in positions at the manager, director and vice president levels, I participated in and led successful initiatives to increase gross profit margins by 2–4 percent and sometimes more through customer focused responsiveness using approaches and techniques described in this book.
2. Proposed by Abraham Maslow in his paper titled "A Theory of Human Motivation," *Psychological Review* 50 (1943): 370–396.
3. This section was first published by the author as "Show Them the Money," *CIO Magazine,* Vol. 19/No. 21, pp. 36–38 15 August 2006.
4. In this book I will most often use the phrase "responsive organization" to name a type of organization that continually senses and responds to changes, threats and opportunities in its environment. However, I also use this name synonymously with other similar names such as "agile enterprise" and "real-time enterprise." There are subtle differences between these names, but there are far more similarities than differences, and this book will focus on those similarities.

CHAPTER 2

Generating Alpha

In the financial investing world, there is an ongoing discussion about something called alpha profits. When investors generate alpha profits, that means they deliver higher returns on their investments than what the market rate of return would normally be, given the riskiness of those investments. Typically, in order to earn higher rates of return, an investor needs to take on higher levels of risk.

However, sometimes investors can earn higher rates of return on lower-risk investments. In these cases, it must be the personal skill of the investors that accounts for the extra return. We all know of investors and fund managers who generate above-market returns year over year for many years running, so their performance is not just luck. Those people have investing and trading strategies that generate alpha profits of 2 to 4 percent above the market rate and sometimes more.

It is also possible for companies to generate profit margins that are 2 to 4 percent (and sometimes more) above the market average for their product or service. These companies have business models that generate alpha business profits. Such companies may or may not have totally new products, but they always find ways to wrap their products in value-added services so that they appeal strongly to customers in targeted market segments.

VALUE-ADDED SERVICES AND ENTREPRENEURIAL EMPLOYEES GENERATE ALPHA

Here's an example based on my experience to illustrate how a company can focus on certain target market customers and use value-added services to customize otherwise commodity products in order to generate alpha profits. Let's call our example company Charlie Supply. Charlie Supply is a company that sells and distributes janitorial supplies and equipment and foodservice disposables. These are common products, and there are many choices available for customers who want to purchase these type of products.

In such a competitive business, how can Charlie Supply ever hope to earn 2 to 4 percent (and sometimes more) greater gross profits than other companies that sell the same products? The answer begins with the fact that Charlie Supply has developed a set of business services that go along with the products it sells. And the company has instituted an ongoing market research and marketing campaign to identify and communicate with those companies most likely to be interested in the combination of its products and its business services. Charlie Supply employees are acting in a very entrepreneurial manner, aren't they?

By targeting customers in these specific market segments instead of just going after the broad market, Charlie Supply can expect to earn higher gross profits because its target customers will pay slightly higher prices in return for a tailored bundle of products and value-added services that best fit their business needs.

The value-added services Charlie Supply has developed are a set of services in the area of supply chain management. The company has invested in systems to support these services and in training their people to deliver them so they excel in this area. When people at Charlie Supply work with a customer, they select the specific mix of these supply chain services needed to meet the customer's exact needs.

They select services such as electronically linking to the customer's order entry system or setting up a customized Web-based product catalog and order entry system for use by the customer's people. They deliver services that tailor how the customer's products are labeled, shipped, and paid for. Charlie Supply can preprocess customer invoices so as to insert the customer's general ledger accounting system codes and send the invoices in an electronic format that allows customers to import these invoices directly into their accounts payable system. The net effect of combining a mix of these services is to create a valuable and customized response to unique and changing customer business needs.

Charlie Supply has created a profile of the kind of customers that would most benefit (and thus be most interested) in its products and supply chain services. It defined these characteristics for companies most likely to benefit from doing business with Charlie Supply:

- Growing revenue and opening up new locations
- Centralizing their procurement function
- Open to outsourcing certain supply chain functions
- The products Charlie Supply sells are mission critical
- Spends a significant portion of their procurement budget on products that Charlie Supply sells
- Making average or above-average profits in their industries

The marketing people at Charlie Supply are focused on finding companies that fit this profile. When they find such companies, they research their needs and find out who the relevant company decision makers are and create a briefing on each company that gets passed along to the sales force. The sales force then uses this research to call on and communicate the value that Charlie Supply can provide these companies.

Charlie Supply is also able to negotiate good prices and sales rebate incentives with manufacturers of the products it sells, so its cost of goods sold is often lower than those of its competitors. Charlie Supply can negotiate these good prices because manufacturers view the company as an important channel to market for their products. Charlie Supply has created a desirable base of customers. Manufacturers want those customers to buy their products, not those of a competitor, so they offer incentives to Charlie Supply to promote their products.

Added to the fact that its sales force is focused on the most profitable customers and its cost of goods sold is very competitive, the company is also able to manage its operating and administrative expenses very well. Its people in those areas are well trained and motivated by performance bonuses they can earn if the company does well. These bonuses are funded by the company's alpha profits. When the company enjoys these profits, the employees who had a hand in creating them also get to share in them.

The net effect of all these different things allows the company to charge slightly higher prices to customers, pay slightly lower prices to manufacturers for the products they sell, and keep their operating expenses slightly lower than those of their competitors. This is how Charlie Supply earns alpha profits of 2 to 4 percent year after year in a very competitive business.

ESCAPE FROM THE TRAP OF COMMODITIZED JOBS

Companies often say their people are their greatest asset, but many of them do not act that way. They treat employees as interchangeable units that can be easily hired and just as easily let go. They do not spend much money on employee training and education because they have made the jobs these people fill into well-regulated routines that do not require high levels of skill. Companies often attempt to put much of the complexity and business problem-solving logic into their computer systems instead of their people so as to capture that knowledge and avoid losing it when they have to downsize their workforce.

Commoditized jobs like this are an example of the industrial assembly-line approach that emphasizes efficiency over responsiveness. This approach tries to define each and every task in detail and then simply have people repeat those tasks over and over without change. This approach worked much better in slower times when conditions stayed the same for longer periods of time and when businesses themselves were much simpler. Yet because many companies cannot think of any other approach, they continue trying to find profits and efficiencies by creating ever more commoditized jobs.

People doing commoditized jobs are not trained to be responsive or to think about creative new ways to do their work—quite the opposite. People in these situations are rewarded for strict conformity to regulations. In fact, people in such jobs who keep suggesting new ways to do things will soon be labeled troublemakers or accused of not being team players.

People in commoditized jobs cannot be paid that much because their jobs do not create that much value; it's a simple fact of life that in business, you cannot pay someone more than they are worth (at least not for long). Another problem is that the experience these workers acquire often does not make them more valuable precisely because their jobs are very defined and regulated so they can be done well enough by a person without a lot of experience. Because of this, there is little opportunity for experienced employees to use their experience in a way that creates more value for the company.

And for people who start out at the modest salaries these jobs can offer, there is still a built-in term limit to their employment at any particular company. This is because, over time, as people in these commoditized jobs get their small annual raises, they start to price themselves out of the salary ranges that these jobs can support. And then they find themselves in the group of employees that gets let go the next time the company goes through a round of downsizing.

These are the built-in traps that play themselves out when companies insist on applying twentieth-century industrial notions of efficiency to the fluid, electronically interconnected global markets of the twenty-first century. From the perspective of efficiency alone, it would seem that people's success in raising their standard of living is the very thing that leads to them losing their jobs. It would seem that there will always be another group of lower-paid workers willing to step in and do their jobs for less.

The answer to this seeming quandary is to realize that efficiency is only one part of the value equation. The other part of the value equation is responsiveness. Responsiveness depends on experience, and it depends on higher levels of training and skill, and it continually increases the value of existing products and services as well as creates new ones. Responsiveness enables people to continually create more value so they also earn the opportunity to be paid more. This is the dynamic that brings forth the entrepreneurial spirit in employees at all levels of a company.

People in North America, Western Europe, and Japan have been struggling with the trap of commoditized jobs for several decades. Now people working in what were once low-wage countries are beginning to feel the effects of market forces as their wages rise. Many countries in the developing regions of the world will soon experience this same phenomenon. It is ironic because we all work hard in order to raise our standards of living, not to remain in low-paid jobs. So the question is: How do we earn and then get to keep the higher standard of living that comes from our hard work?

WELCOME TO THE FIRST WORLD—NOW YOUR LABOR RATES ARE TOO HIGH

Countries that only 10 to 15 years ago were outsourcing destinations because of their low labor costs are now achieving first-world status. Ireland is one such country that is now going through the same transitions people have been going through in the United States and other parts of Europe for the last few decades.

Fifteen years ago Ireland was a destination country for outsourcing IT services, customer support, and administrative and clerical services. The country's economy has since prospered; Irish labor rates have risen, and now companies are moving some operations to other lower-wage countries, such as India, Eastern Europe, China, and elsewhere.

The global economy is getting better and better and faster and faster at moving work to places where the greatest value is created at the lowest cost. Soon standard labor rates for a broad range of services will be in effect globally; they'll be set and constantly updated by the forces of supply and demand in the global economy.

The more you can standardize and commoditize an activity or service, the easier it is to outsource it and move it from one country to another to take advantage of lower labor costs. This happened in manufacturing and it's happening again with services such as customer support, IT operations, accounting, and general administrative services.

But things can happen in our electronically interconnected economy that could not happen in the older industrial economy. People often do not need to congregate at a central place called a factory or an office any more to do many types of work; they can work from anywhere and collaborate in virtual teams. Teams of workers can operate from North America, or Europe, or Asia, or anywhere that has a good broadband Internet connection. The same high-speed global networks that make outsourcing possible also enable workers to be physically located in any country.

And these networks of people have much more flexibility; they can respond as economies change and labor rates shift. This flexibility means labor rates will fluctuate. Of course, it is not easy for some workers to see the value of their labor go from $80 an hour to $20 an hour as labor rates change, but it doesn't necessarily mean they have to lose their jobs.

NEW OPPORTUNITIES TO CREATE VALUE

If people go with the flow, $20 an hour is still better than unemployment, and they have the option to learn new skills for jobs that the global market values at higher rates. What are those better-paying jobs? They are often jobs that require a mix of technical and business skills where practitioners work very closely with other businesspeople. They design and develop new products or services along with the systems needed to bring them to market.

These are the better paying jobs because many (maybe even most) opportunities for companies to make a profit now involve being super-responsive to specific categories of customers and continuously updating their existing products and creating new ones to meet customers' changing circumstances and desires. In the global real-time economy, responsiveness trumps efficiency; business agility is the key to success. And people who make responsiveness happen generate more value and create opportunities to earn more money.

An example of the ability of responsiveness to transform the operations and increase the profits of even the most traditional kinds of businesses is provided by a clothing retailer named Zara (www.zara.com), which started out in Spain and has now spread all through Europe and into North and South America and Asia. It has developed a highly responsive business model and needs only four to six weeks to develop and get new fashions to its stores, where the industry average is nine months. Zara can launch thousands of new fashions in a year; its competitors are hard-pressed to introduce more than four or five new fashions.[1]

Instead of relying on just a few designers and hoping they come up with fashions that will appeal to a broad market, Zara has an in-house group of several hundred designers who develop clothes based on popular fashions and who create their own new fashions. These designers have the opportunity to get much closer to the customers who buy their clothes, and they can quickly detect emerging new customer trends. This detection of new trends is backed up by the company's ability to quickly deliver new fashions to its stores based on its responsive network of factories and warehouses and its use of customized production and inventory control systems to drive that network.

Because of its emphasis on responsiveness, Zara has also not participated in the usual industry practice of transferring all production to low-cost-labor countries. Its business model allows workers to create enough value so that their jobs do not need to be eliminated. Zara uses a model where factories coordinate closely with the stores they support in order to produce and deliver the quick fashion changes that customers find so attractive. Zara finds it valuable to locate its factories closer to the retail stores they support.

RESPONSIVENESS ENABLES A HIGHER STANDARD OF LIVING

There is an inexorable global process now sorting out various jobs and skills.[2] Certain jobs—the ones that are more standardized and routine—have become commoditized, and their value has declined because there is a much greater supply of people who can do those jobs. White-collar jobs, such as standard accounting work, routine financial analysis, standard market research and demographic analysis, and all sorts of routine customer service activities, are being done in countries with lower cost of labor.

People who formerly did these jobs at higher pay rates in first-world countries are seeing their jobs disappear; they need to find opportunities to do work where they can add more value to the products or services they create. Opportunities for higher-value work lie in the responsive organization. It is work related to the continuous enhancement of a company's existing products and the delivery of new products. As presented in Chapter 1, much of this work is related to the wrapping of commodity products in a blanket of value-added services to customize them for the needs of individual customers.

People pay a few percentage points more to get products and services customized just so to fit their unique needs, and responsive companies find ways to meet these needs as they evolve more effectively—and often less expensively—than their traditional competitors. It is in the creation of this alpha profit that people will find the opportunity to do work that creates more value and enables them to earn higher incomes once again.

FIX THE OPPORTUNITY GAP

Over time, money tends to concentrate in the hands of fewer and fewer people. And when there is not a broad middle class in a country, there is also much more social and political instability, so it is desirable for countries to have a healthy middle class. In attempting to address this problem, people have naturally focused on the income gap between the average worker and those at the top of the income scale, and they have proposed many plans to redistribute income.

Perhaps another way to address this problem is to focus on fixing the opportunity gap and see if the income gap would start to adjust on its own. People at the top of the income scale almost always have a much greater opportunity to create value (and thus earn more) than people at the middle or lower end of the scale.[3] What would happen if we looked at ways to redistribute opportunity instead of money?

People trapped in commoditized jobs clearly have little opportunity to increase the value of their work, and that limits the amount of money they can earn. If they could find opportunities to create more value, they would see their income increase. Most people are ready, willing, and able to work hard, learn new skills, and try new things. But they cannot find opportunities where they can apply this pent-up energy of theirs.

Now consider how the responsive organization creates value. It creates value because it finds ways to continuously adjust to changing economic circumstances and evolving customer needs. Doing this requires that everybody in an organization be involved in a process of continuous improvement and change. What would motivate people to pay this much attention to their jobs and take the time to constantly learn new skills and develop new products?

We already know the answer to that question. The kind of behavior that the responsive organization depends on is what we call entrepreneurial behavior, and it happens when people have the opportunity to enjoy the rewards and the income associated with their hard work. If there are no rewards (or only threats), then people will simply not be motivated to do what it takes.

So the answer is to encourage entrepreneurial behavior by the distribution of opportunities to people to earn more money when the company they work for earns more money. The opportunity to earn additional profits motivates company owners to work hard and take risks and learn new skills and develop new products. The responsive organization comes into being when this opportunity (and this motivation) is available to everyone in the organization.

A Different Way of Working

A well-documented example in the United States of a company that has used this approach and benefited handsomely from doing so is a company named Springfield Remanufacturing Corporation (www.srcreman.com).[4] For the last 25 years, it has been evolving and perfecting a business model that distributes the opportunity to earn more money to everyone in the company. It has created a range of businesses from a single starting company, and all of these businesses are companies where people behave like entrepreneurs to their own and their organizations' benefit.

Everyone in these organizations, from brand-new hires on up, learns to read the financial statements. Everybody learns to read income statements, balance sheets, and cash flow reports. And everyone gets these reports every week, summarized for the whole company and in detail for their particular business unit or department. So they know what is going on. They use this understanding to participate in setting the financial performance goals for their business unit. Instead of one person or a small group of executives deciding what the company should do, there is a process that involves everyone in setting performance goals and operating plans.

People buy into company goals because they participate in setting them. They also have a personal stake in achieving those goals because they earn performances bonuses every quarter based on reaching these goals. Depending on their position in the company, that is how they can earn an additional 13 to 25 percent of their base pay. The value of their stock options also rises when their company does well. Over the last 25 years, the company has diversified and grown steadily from sales of about $10 million to sales of around $300 million.

Another well-documented example of this kind of company is a company in Brazil called Semco SA (http://semco.locaweb.com.br/en/).[5] Semco has also been practicing and refining a different way of working over the last 25 years. The approach it used and its results have been quite similar to those results produced at Springfield Remanufacturing Corporation. Semco uses a very decentralized business model where employees are deeply involved in setting company goals and are given authority to decide and act to achieve their objectives without waiting for permission. Everyone in the company has access to company financial reports at all times so they have a clear picture of what is happening in the company and how effective their own actions are.

Semco has also diversified from a single line into a group of related lines of business. In each one it has expertise and can distinguish and differentiate itself from competitors by adding extra value to products.

(Semco does not compete by being the lowest-price provider.) It places an emphasis on partnering with other companies to get into new markets, and it has grown steadily in spite of the economic difficulties experienced by Brazil in the last two decades. Over the last 25 years, Semco has grown from sales of $4 million to sales in excess of $200 million.

Both of these companies were born when new management took over troubled organizations in declining industries. In both cases, new management instituted what seemed like radical procedures as a way of enabling the company to respond to challenges that would otherwise drive it out of business. People felt the fire at their backs; they knew they could only go forward; and to do that, they had to try something significantly different from the procedures that had gotten them into their dire circumstances in the first place.

The Great Game of Business

How can people be motivated to transform the way they participate in that activity we all call work? Business has been using the team metaphor for some time now, yet it is rare to see the kind of real teamwork and team spirit in business that we all respond to when we watch a winning sports team rise to the challenge and clinch a championship. The good news is that the answer is staring us right in the face. We are social creatures, we love to play games, and business is a game.

It is through playing games that we all began to learn when we were babies and children. It is through games that we will learn what we need to know to thrive in the real-time world. The game analogy to business is actually much more accurate than the war or battle analogy. The use of the word "game" in no way trivializes or minimizes the seriousness of the undertaking. Ask any professional golfer or basketball player or soccer player; they know full well how serious a game is.

When people have a personal stake in the outcome of a game, they become interested in that game. When people are interested in something, they pay attention and learn quickly. I am always amazed when people who might at first appear not to be very well educated or not to know very much can suddenly tell me volumes when a subject arises that interests them. People can reel off names and statistics about their favorite teams, they can guide me through the intricacies of reading a racing form that describes the horses and riders in a race, or they can tell me everything about the history and most likely future behaviors of the characters in a soap opera. People can create fantasy sports teams by combining players just as skillfully as a mutual funds manager creates a winning portfolio by combining stocks of different companies.

Senior managers and entrepreneurs already know how to play the great game of business because they all have significant reasons to be very interested and to become very knowledgeable about it. To be a successful real-time enterprise, everybody in the organization needs to have a keen interest in the organization's performance, and they must constantly be learning to improve their own performance and that of the organization. Any company can acquire and install technology; for this reason, technology alone cannot constitute a significant or long-lasting competitive advantage. Sustainable advantage comes only from the skill of the players and the way they play the game.

In his book *The Great Game of Business*,[6] Jack Stack describes how to start and sustain a responsive company. I would summarize his ideas into four basic conditions that must exist for responsiveness to occur, and they are:

1. People must understand the rules of the game and how it is played; they must know what is fair and what is not fair and how to score points.

2. They need to get the training and experience necessary to keep developing skills to succeed and advance in their chosen jobs.

3. All players must know what the score is at all times; they need to know if they are winning or losing and see the results of their actions.

4. All players must have a personal stake in the outcome; there must be some important reward (usually monetary) that provides a reason for each player to strive to succeed.

PROFIT POTENTIAL OF THE SELF-ADJUSTING FEEDBACK LOOP

The great game of business creates and sustains what is known as a self-adjusting feedback loop within an organization. The self-adjusting feedback loop is a very useful phenomenon. An example of such a loop is the cruise control in an automobile. The cruise control constantly reads the vehicle's actual speed and compares that to the speed it was set for. It responds so as to bring the actual speed in line with the desired speed, causing the engine to accelerate or decelerate. The cruise control's goal is to achieve and maintain the desired speed. As the vehicle travels down the highway, the cruise control continuously monitors speed and operates the engine to achieve its goal.

Other examples of a self-adjusting feedback loop at work are a thermostat that controls the temperature in a room or a guided missile that zeroes in on a heat source or a radar emission source. Self-adjusting feedback loops use balancing feedback (known as negative feedback in engineering circles) to continuously adjust and correct their behavior. Balancing feedback[7] occurs when a system compares its current state with its desired state (or goal) and takes corrective action to move it in a direction that will minimize the difference between the two states. A continuous stream of balancing feedback guides a system (or a company) through a changing environment toward its goal.

Companies can learn to constantly adjust their behavior day after day, hour by hour, to respond to events and continue to steer toward their performance targets. The opportunity now exists to leverage the power of the self-adjusting feedback loop within companies and across groups of companies doing business together. Real-time data sharing and close coordination between companies can be employed to deliver otherwise unobtainable operating efficiencies.

One of the most effective ways to harness the power of feedback loops is to cast people's interactions with each other in the form of a game, a game whose object is to achieve a goal specified by particular performance targets. If people in a company have real-time access to their performance data, then they see the results of their actions and learn to coordinate their actions so as to steer toward their targets. If they are rewarded when they achieve their targets, then they will learn to hit those targets more often than not. Now the profit potential of the self-adjusting feedback loop is unleashed—this is how alpha is generated.

TOWARD A RESPONSIVE BUSINESS OPERATING STRATEGY

Our economy is in a period of major structural change. Whole industries are changing and markets are placing value in new areas. Companies need to keep in touch with what their markets value and find ways to deliver goods and services in a most cost-effective way. This economic necessity is the mother of business invention, and successful companies are those that learn to constantly evolve new ways of doing things.

New businesses are always in need of new or modified information systems to support their evolving operations procedures. So the ability to modify existing systems and deliver new systems in a timely manner is central to a company's ability to be responsive.

For the last 30 years or so, strategies for using information technology often involved massive multiyear projects to replace or roll out whole new systems. The failure rate on these projects has been consistently in the neighborhood of 70 to 80 percent.[8] And those systems that are delivered often do not meet expectations, or they restrict what people can do by imposing cumbersome work procedures on them. Companies clearly need a less risky and more flexible way to use IT and deliver new systems.

From years of experience (and learning the hard way at times), I have found that the most effective strategy for creating responsive business operations is to automate the routine operations and only the routine operations. Most activities in any business are 80 to 90 percent routine, and those are the activities to standardize and automate as much as possible. This is where you focus relentlessly on efficiency and low cost. But resist the temptation to create complex systems to handle the unique or nonroutine activities because that extra complexity will become expensive and will bog you down.

It is also pointless to automate that part of the business since it is the part that often changes the fastest. Thus, even if you do succeed in automating it, the rules and process logic will soon change, and all that work will be for naught.

Instead, empower people to handle the unique and nonroutine situations. You want people in the loop when something unexpected happens; you don't want artificial intelligence. You want real intelligence, you want people (who have a stake in the outcome) in there watching what's going on and figuring out how to respond. This is what people do very, very well; we humans have a brain that is still the best problem solver and innovator this planet has ever seen. No computer (no matter how expensive and complex) can even come close.

USE PEOPLE AND COMPUTERS EACH FOR THEIR STRENGTHS

Use computers to do what they do best. Let them handle the day-in, day-out moving of routine data related to basic transactions such as purchase orders, invoices, account balances, order status, address changes, and so on. Wherever there are people doing routine data entry or repetitious work of any sort, this is an opportunity to automate. Computers do this sort of work much better, faster, and cheaper.

Use people to do what they do best. What they do best is think, communicate, and solve problems. We don't need to build lots of intelligence, complexity, and cost into new computer systems if we free up people from routine work and give them the data and training they need to solve complex problems and handle the exceptions to routine operations. We don't need artificial intelligence in our systems when we can apply the real intelligence of people who are trained, motivated, and empowered.

The opportunity is for companies to really maximize the use of the information technology they already have. It means developing new systems by leveraging the capabilities and features of existing systems. This can be done by building data links between existing systems and creating simple user interfaces that blend together functions from existing systems. (This concept is known as service-oriented architecture or SOA.)

So how do you get started? Think of a new, more cost-efficient and more responsive way to perform an existing business operation; or think of a brand-new business operation needed to support a new market opportunity. This isn't rocket science. Ask people who work in your business operating units. They already know of opportunities and ways to do their jobs better.

Then think of features from your company's existing systems that could be combined in new ways to support these new business processes. Now challenge your IT people to use as many features as possible from existing systems to create the new system you have in mind. By challenging your IT people in this way, you will be able to get a new system built faster and with less programming. (See examples of this in Chapter 5.)

Resist the temptation to build lots of complexity into the new systems. Remember, automate the routine and free people up to handle the exceptions—that's the creative work. Most business operations are routine and repetitive work that can be handled with a very simple set of processing rules. Focus on automating that work.

"But what about the nonroutine stuff?" you ask. Here's what to do. Whenever a transaction happens that does not follow one of the simple routine processing rules, have the system just trap the data related to that transaction and notify a qualified person. Deliver the data to the people who fix exceptions to the general rules and let them take it from there. The computer then returns to processing the vast majority of transactions that are routine.

People will either be able to correct the data so that it fits back into a simple predefined process or they will take care of the transactions themselves all the way through. They will have time to do this because they won't be bogged down and worn out doing the routine stuff. And this is where they can generate the most value for customers and for the company (also known as generating alpha profits).

And these people will do a great job too. Since it is nonroutine, it is interesting. It will involve thinking, communicating with others, and problem solving. People like doing this kind of work. It's fun. The human brain is more fine-tuned than any computer to do just this kind of work.

By automating the mass of rote, routine, and repetitious work, your organization will get great cost efficiencies. By empowering people to handle all the nonroutine stuff, companies will become very responsive to unique customer needs. It is this blend of efficiency and responsiveness that will enable a company to outperform its competition.

By using this strategy, your business will avoid spending large amounts of money to solve problems that will themselves soon change. They will be able to move fast and exploit new opportunities as they present themselves.

By the time your slower-moving and more traditional competitors finally roll out their new systems, the game will have changed, customer desires and market opportunities will have moved on, and your company will also have moved on.

NOTES

1. "Zara: Taking the Lead in Fast-Fashion," *BusinessWeek*, 4 April 2006. http://www.businessweek.com/globalbiz/content/apr2006/gb20060404_167078.htm?chan=innovation_branding_brand+profiles.
2. Thomas Friedman has described this global economic process in great detail in his book *The World is Flat* (New York: Picador, 2007); see Chapter 2, "The Ten Forces That Flattened the World."
3. An insightful exploration of this familiar pattern is offered by Mark Buchanan in his book *Nexus: Small Worlds and the Ground Breaking Science of Networks* (New York: W.W. Norton & Company, 2002); see Chapter 7, "The Rich Get Richer."
4. Jack Stack, *The Great Game of Business* (New York: Currency/Doubleday, 1992). See Chapter 4, "The Big Picture."
5. Ricardo Semler, *Maverick: The Success Story Behind the World's Most Unusual Workplace* (New York: Grand Central Publishing, 1995).
6. Stack, *The Great Game of Business*; See Chapter 1, "Why We Teach People How to Make Money" and Chapter 10, "A Company of Owners."
7. I am using notions of balancing feedback loops and reinforcing feedback loops as they are described by Peter Senge in his book *The Fifth Discipline: The Art & Practice of the Learning Organization* (New York: Doubleday Business, 2006); see Chapter 5, "A Shift of Mind."
8. CHAOS Report by the Standish Group, Ipswitch, MA. (http://www.standishgroup.com/); they summarize their ongoing IT industry research every two years in a report called the CHAOS Report; the most recent such report came out in 2006.

CHAPTER **3**

Principles of the Responsive Organization

As the realities of the relentlessly competitive, real time economy continue to sink in, more and more people realize that making their companies agile and responsive to continuous change will be the best way for them to compete in their markets. Unless a company is the low price leader in its industry, competing on price and efficiency alone will not be enough to succeed. Companies realize their greatest asset is the customers they sell to, and the best way to grow and enhance that asset is to stay in constant touch with those customers and keep changing as their customers change.

Responsiveness means being aware of market trends and evolving customer desires. Responsive companies listen carefully to what customers say; they watch what sells and what does not; and they are always on the lookout for opportunities to modify existing products and services or introduce brand-new products and services. And when they see their opportunities, they act. They don't dither. They know time is of the essence.

MORE COORDINATION, LESS CONTROL

Let's talk about what it means to be responsive and agile. There's a right way and a wrong way to do it, and often the right way seems counterintuitive at first . . . until you get the hang of it.

The counterintuitive part is that to be agile and responsive, a company has to place *less* controls on people, not more. Because people need to move more quickly and need to coordinate more closely with each other, we tend to think this requires more control to keep everything moving. So we create pyramid-shape organization structures where all-powerful executives sit in the top boxes and call the shots while everyone else is supposed to just carry out their orders.

The problem is that this kind of centralized control structure never works in a fast-paced environment. People at the top of the pyramids are too far removed from the scene of the action, and it takes too long for them to understand what is happening and to make good decisions. People in this position inevitably find themselves becoming bottlenecks because there are too many decisions requiring their input and they cannot keep up with the pace of events. Instead of more control, what companies need is more *coordination*.

Coordination happens when people are motivated to work together. And the best way to motivate people to work together is to reward them with something they all want that requires them to work together to obtain. In return for rewards, senior managers can define performance objectives they want their people to reach and then leave it to them to figure out the details. Because people have the opportunity to think for themselves, and because they have the motivation of rewards, they learn fast and figure out ways to achieve their objectives.

Give people the skills training and the equipment they need but resist the urge to tell them how to do their jobs. When people are motivated, they figure things out, and as they do so, they get better and better at their work. As a result, an organization becomes more aware, more responsive, and more effective—it achieves its performance targets more and more often. This is how responsiveness and agility happen; it's the effect of many people coordinating with each other moment to moment and week to week to reach common goals.

A Case Study in What Works and What Does Not

To illustrate this idea, let's look at two companies that are each trying to become more responsive to their fast-changing and demanding markets. The first company—we'll call it Trying-Hard Corporation—has decided to reorganize its many different operating units into three new centralized divisions so as to become more nimble, reduce bureaucracy, and better compete with its rivals. The three divisions will focus on, respectively, the company's customers, the company's internal operations, and the enabling technology that the company uses to run its business.

The company's chief executive announced, "There is no question, our new structure will increase accountability, will reduce bottlenecks, and speed decision making." The CEO further stated that there will be management changes below the company's top ranks and gave as an example a vice president who was formerly responsible for one product line who will now get additional responsibilities for three or four other product lines. (And of course the vice presidents who used to head up those other product lines will be let go.)

The increased concentration of responsibilities under this vice president is one example of how the company is seeking to "eliminate red tape and enable people to move faster." It seems like Trying-Hard is taking the right steps to jump-start operations and be responsive. But then, perhaps, it might also be doing something that will only make its problems worse.

Trying-Hard Corporation is increasing control instead of increasing coordination. It is going for the old industrial approach of cutting operating expenses and reducing the number of higher-paid staff through centralizing operations so as to get better economies of scale. This will make the company more efficient, but now it is in danger of getting even more efficient at doing the same things that got it into trouble in the first place.

Where will ideas for new products and services come from? In the newly centralized (and downsized) environment, people will be keeping their heads down and trying to avoid getting fired. Nobody is going to be in a mood to try something new or different or do anything at all without first getting approval all the way up the chain of command. Act with caution will be the order of the day; the people at the top of the three new divisions

(continued)

will find themselves frantically busy; and everybody else will be waiting around for them to make decisions. This is not the way to be responsive.

Another company, we'll call it Getting-Results Company, is responding to the challenges it faces by increasing its ability to coordinate instead of to control. Getting-Results has decided to embark on an experiment to transform its culture, a culture that until now has been known for long hours and micromanaging bosses. The endeavor, called ROWE, for "results-only work environment," seeks to demolish decades-old company dogma that equates employees' physical presence with productivity. The intention is now to judge people's performance based on output instead of the number of hours they put in at the office.

The idea is that it doesn't make much difference where you are anymore in this wireless connected world. Except for face-to-face meetings, people can do the rest of their work anywhere and anytime they want. As long as they meet their delivery deadlines and hit their performance targets, people can schedule their work to suit their personal needs. That means come in late or not at all some days; take off in the middle of the day to go bike riding; or work from home at two o'clock in the morning if they want.

It also turns out that this idea was hatched in the ranks of middle management, not senior management. (These ideas often happen first in middle management ranks because people there are closest to the action and feel the pressure to do something more strongly than senior management.) After ROWE was quietly tried and succeeded in several of the company's operating units, it came to the attention of the company CEO, who backed the idea of implementing it throughout the organization. The company's experience shows that ROWE delivers compelling results even though there are lots of doubters and political obstacles still in its way.

One general manager in another business unit that was about to implement the ROWE program was not supportive at first and was terrified about the loss of control. He kept asking "How are you going to measure this so you know you're getting the same productivity out of people?"

Everyone agreed that if performance started to slip, the experiment would be called off. The company installed business intelligence and process management systems so business unit managers and unit employees could see the productivity of their unit and the company as a whole. Within a couple of months, people started to see that not only was productivity up, but customer satisfaction scores were also the highest they had ever been.

People in the different business units of Getting-Results started engaging with each other and coordinating to get things done, not because they were ordered to do so but because they got a big personal reward for doing so. They got to take back control of their time instead of living under the tyranny of logging endless hours at the office. And because they got more control over their lives, they were more satisfied with their jobs, and they got more done, and they took better care of the company's customers too.

As the world and the company's customers continue to change, people at Getting-Results Company will continue to figure out how to respond and how to excel so they can continue to enjoy the reward of being in control of their time. This is a powerful responsive dynamic, and the company will reap the rewards it brings.

END OF CONTROL AS WE KNOW IT—THE DYNAMICS OF SWARMING

If traditional notions of control are no longer as effective as they once were, where can we look to find examples of the kind of decentralized coordination that we can use in business? Researchers and practitioners are beginning to notice a very powerful example for this kind of coordination; they find it as they study the behavior of flocks of birds and schools of fish.

What makes a flock of birds or school of fish move as if they are a single entity? What makes all the individuals suddenly rise, turn, and accelerate at the same time? There is something else at work here than just a leader bird or a captain fish telling all the others what to do. The organization of a flock or school is not a hierarchy, it is a network. The quick coordinated behavior from large groups of individuals in these networks is called swarming.

Swarming might also call to mind seemingly negative images of killer bees or fire ants, but consider those images from the perspective of the bee or the ant. In their swarming behavior they are not just members of some clumsy hierarchy waiting around to be told what to do. Instead, they act fast on their own initiative and their opponents must either flee or else be overwhelmed. What if our companies could act this quickly and effectively?

Swarms place more emphasis on decentralized coordination than on centralized control to get things done. We are used to the hierarchical, top-down model of centralized control, but this model is proving to be too rigid, too slow moving, too cumbersome to deliver the responsiveness we now need. So how can we use the example of quick coordination that we see in swarms to guide our companies' behavior?

A Rich Opportunity Awaits Us

Consider this: What could happen if managers made performance objectives very clear and understandable to everybody in a company and then started streaming real-time performance data to dashboards displayed on people's PCs, laptops, and mobile phones? Everybody in a company would be able to see a real-time picture of the operations they are responsible for, and they could see when their unit's performance started to drift outside of desired operating parameters. Then they could quickly drill down to access relevant information needed to respond quickly and effectively.

When everyone knows what their objectives or performance targets are and when they can see moment to moment what is going on and whether their operations are on target or off target, something powerful starts to happen. Swarming behavior emerges as people learn how their individual actions combine to create larger effects. Those larger effects are the organizational responses that move their company toward achieving its performance targets even as the world continues to change. This is swarming behavior in a company. It is fast, powerful, and continuously responsive to change.

People using swarming techniques can bring about organizational behavior that yields continuous efficiency and profitability from a thousand small adjustments and some occasional big wins. When customer service people start working together more effectively with salespeople, and salespeople start working more effectively with operations people, and information technology people start working more effectively with everybody, then amazing things happen.

Swarming behavior depends on decentralization of information and delegation of authority. Decentralization of information allows people to see how their individual actions relate to overall company performance. Decentralization of control is accomplished by giving everyone a clear set of performance targets that they are motivated to achieve. Those performance targets define the results that are expected of them, but people have authority to figure out for themselves how to deliver those results.

The speed and efficiency demanded of responsive organizations can occur only if people think for themselves and control their own actions; the notion that some central person (or computer) can do all the thinking for everybody else is a quaint idea from the days of the industrial revolution. It worked in a slower, simpler, more predictable world, but it does not work now.

Most companies still use traditional hierarchical organization models. They employ centralized command and control systems, and most employees still have their work closely regulated by supervisors and bosses. These companies focus on traditional industrial concepts of economies of scale and operating efficiencies achieved through rigorous application of standard operating procedures. In these circumstances there is little incentive for anyone except senior managers to take any initiative or to try anything different from the norm. People simply do as they are told and little more.

Many of us are still wedded to the notion that top-down command and control is the most effective way to run big companies and get complex things done. This deeply held belief is based on the time-honored notion that the traditional pyramid-shape hierarchy is the most logical and efficient way to structure an organization and manage work. Workers report to managers; managers report to directors; directors report to vice presidents; and vice presidents report to a person known as the Big Cheese (see Figure 3.1).

For many people (myself included), the idea of a responsive organization at first seems like just a speeded-up version of the traditional hierarchy. I used to think a responsive organization is what we would get if we took the aeronautic controls and heads-up data display out of the cockpit of a jet fighter and installed them on the boss's desk. Then we

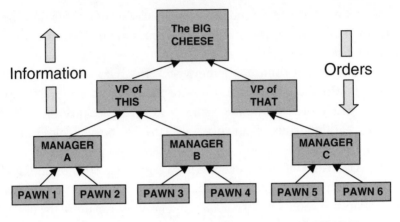

Centrally controlled hierarchies move <u>too</u> <u>SLOWLY</u>.

FIGURE 3.1   Business as Usual

could hook up a high-powered database to collect all sorts of information from all over the company and run the data through the heads-up display. The boss would know everything right away and could issue orders to everybody real fast—right?

Notions like swarming behavior violate our classic concepts of command and control; they sound pretty chaotic. We might agree that swarming behavior could work when objectives are simple and short term. But for more complex and long-term objectives, we tend to believe we need complex management and control procedures. We believe that decentralization of control would not be time or resource efficient. So many complex interdependencies exist between different activities; how could anyone except a central supreme commander sort them all out?

Networks Work Better than Hierarchies in Complex Environments

Let me respond to these beliefs with a story from an economics professor I once studied with. He would start his story by saying there were once two contending points of view about how to best organize and control a nation's economy. And, of course, controlling a nation's economy certainly involves a lot of complex interdependencies to sort out, and it is a long-term project.

He went on to say one point of view held that a centrally controlled, rationally organized economy directed by experts was the best way to deal with all the complex issues. (This is the classic pyramid-shape hierarchy.) He said the other point of view believed all that was needed was a central group to coordinate and enforce a clear set of rules and regulations, such as respect for contracts and honest reporting of financial activities. That central group must provide clear rules and regulations that are effective and it must rigorously enforce them and ensure that honest reporting of financial activities actually does happen. Otherwise no further involvement from them was needed, because people and companies could organize and control themselves without further intervention. (This is a swarming network.)

Then he described how a high-level delegation from the government of a developing country tried to figure out which of these two models to adopt. First they traveled to New York City and visited the trading floor of the New York Stock Exchange. It was a chaotic crowd scene; people were running about writing things on scraps of paper; they were shouting at each other, waving their arms, making hand signals; and the walls were covered with huge computer screens and electronic displays showing a constantly changing barrage of numbers and words.

Next, the delegation traveled to the former Soviet Union and visited the Ministry of Economic Planning. They saw buildings filled with rows of orderly desks; well-educated scientists, engineers, and economists collected information; and the ministry made plans and issued orders for what each sector of the economy should produce and when and how much would be needed in order to meet the nation's development goals. Which model do you think the delegation recommended to their government when they returned home from their travels?

The notion that some central person or group can do all the thinking for everybody else and tell them what to do and how to do it is fundamentally flawed. No amount of centralized reporting and planning systems and computing power can adequately process the amount of data that needs to be processed in the short time frames now required. The answer lies in breaking up the data to be processed and the decisions to be made into many smaller jobs that can all run simultaneously—this is swarming dynamics. It is similar to the concepts used in the design of massively parallel computer networks. (The Internet itself is a massively parallel network.)

Companies that employ decentralized control structures, that incentivize and train their people to think and act for themselves and provide them with the real-time performance data they need to make good decisions, will outperform their competitors. This is because people working in self-directed teams striving to achieve common performance objectives find hundreds of ways to make continuous small adjustments that increase their profits and decrease their costs every day, every week, every month.

These companies benefit from a continuous stream of efficiencies generated by many small, rapid adjustments as business situations change. They also benefit from profits gained by avoiding threats or quickly responding to market opportunities as they appear.

Walk through any company; talk to people in the operating units; ask them if they know ways to make their activities more productive and ways to save more money. Ask them if they know ways to better serve customers and if they have ideas for new products or services that customers would want. In most cases people will answer yes to all these questions.

What would happen if these people had clear performance objectives and authority to figure out for themselves how to achieve those objectives? What would happen if they received a constant stream of data from systems that showed them the results of their actions and whether they were acting effectively or not? How fast would people learn to act on their own initiative and be more productive, save money, increase customer service, and offer new products and services?

Organizational swarming behavior causes an organization to act as a single coordinated entity. An apt analogy for this is the human body; it can be seen as a swarm of cells that continually sense their environment and act on their own without waiting to be told what to do. Our brains

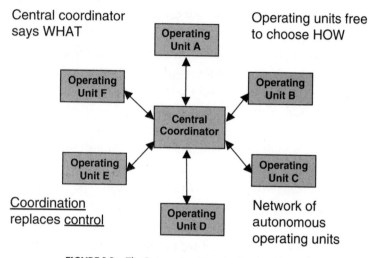

FIGURE 3.2   The Responsive Organization Is a Network

are not aware of everything that our bodies are doing, nor do they need to be; individual cells and organs know how to act on their own. And the overall effect of these swarming cells is to produce the coordinated behavior that makes our lives possible.

Unlike the slower and more predictable industrial economy of the twentieth century, we live in an unpredictable global economy. The best efficiencies come from swarming dynamics that make hundreds of small adjustments to respond quickly as situations change. Organizations operating like this are structured as networks of many self-directed operating units that respond quickly without waiting to be told what to do (see Figure 3.2).[1]

LEADERSHIP FOR THE RESPONSIVE ORGANIZATION

There are two kinds of leadership; one depends on orders and supervision; the other depends on training and trust. One kind of leadership values control; the other kind values responsiveness. If you are trying to create a responsive organization, which kind of leadership would you use?

The first kind of leadership is what we are most familiar with. It is where the person in charge tells people what to do and watches to make sure they do as they are told. It is leadership characterized by high visibility, issuing orders, and getting personally involved in lots of details. This style of leadership is needed when people aren't sure what to do. This is *explicit* leadership because it is exact and unequivocal; people are expected to listen carefully and then do as they are told.

The other kind of leadership is *implicit* leadership. This style is characterized by leaders who adopt a low profile, who seek consensus, and who delegate details to others. Leaders who use this style are clear about what they want, but they do not say how they want it done. They provide their people with lots of training and let them decide how to do what has been asked of them. People are trusted to figure things out for themselves.

The responsive organization is an organization that can handle high-change situations, that can assess new situations quickly and then act fast to achieve its goals. You would think explicit leadership is what you need to create responsiveness and agility. Yet actually, *implicit* leadership is what you need. This does not seem right at first, but think about it.

In my experience, explicit leadership works for only a short time (usually not more than 12 months) before people start to turn off; "leader fatigue" sets in. Explicit leaders work harder and harder for less and less response. People become numb; they don't think for themselves; they do nothing at all unless told to. This is not agile behavior. Explicit leadership becomes like welfare; over time it robs people of their drive and self-initiative.

Explicit leadership has its place, but it is effective only for short periods. The question then becomes how to use implicit leadership most of the time, even though we live in a fast-paced world where situations are always changing. Don't confuse implicit leadership with slow, bureaucratic managerial practices or with leadership by committee. There is actually a very active side to implicit leadership, but it is more in the nature of teaching and encouraging people to think and act for themselves instead of telling them what to do. As the saying goes, give people a fish and they will eat tonight, but teach them to fish and they will eat for life.

Responsiveness is a way of working, not just a passing fad. And implicit leadership is the best style of leadership for organizations over the long haul. Implicit leadership starts by setting meaningful goals that are clear and stable. Meaningful goals are statements of intent; they are descriptions of what an organization strives to accomplish. They do not change even though the situations an organization encounters change all the time. When goals and the performance objectives needed to achieve those goals are clear, people understand what is expected of them and become skilled at figuring out how to achieve those goals.

When people learn to think and act for themselves without waiting to be told what to do, they can be agile. Although it may seem slow at first, implicit leadership is what fosters responsiveness in an organization.[2]

DYNAMICS OF THE RESPONSIVE ORGANIZATION

Three essential process or feedback loops combine to bring the responsive organization to life (see Figure 3.3). The first loop, Loop 1, is for

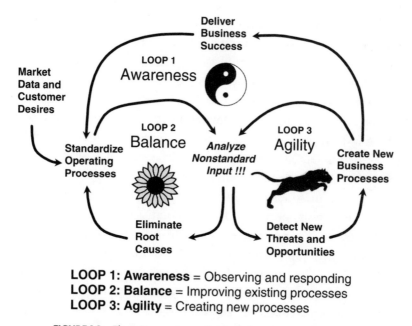

LOOP 1: Awareness = Observing and responding
LOOP 2: Balance = Improving existing processes
LOOP 3: Agility = Creating new processes

FIGURE 3.3 Three Process Loops Drive the Responsive Organization

observing the environment and deciding what needs to be done. We'll call this the "Awareness" process within the organization. People in Loop 1 are the ones who decide *what* to do. They are responsible for understanding the company's markets and making decisions about how the company will position itself and participate in these markets. They decide what the company needs to do to achieve the success it desires.

Strategy happens in Loop 1, and tactics happen in Loops 2 and 3. So, clearly, the activities that occur in Loop 1 are central to the success of any organization, because if they are not done well—if good strategies are not decided upon—then the actions carried out in Loops 2 and 3 will not be effective. No amount of tactical excellence can compensate for flawed strategy. We'll talk more about the Loop 1 process of awareness in the next two chapters.

Once a decision is made, one or both of the other two process loops are engaged to act on that decision. People in these processes are the ones who decide *how* something will be done. Loop 2 is for improving existing operations. People in this loop find and fix root cause problems in business processes that generate errors and thus create nonstandard input; this is what delivers operating efficiency. We'll call it the "Balance" process because it requires people to constantly adjust and fine-tune standard operating procedures so as to get the best overall performance as operating conditions change. This process is continuous; it happens all the time, every day.

Loop 3 is for creating new operations. People here design and build new procedures and systems to deal with the appearance of something new—a new threat or a new opportunity. That is what delivers effectiveness. We'll call this process "Agility" because it requires people to move quickly when situations call for it. Creating something new is different from the process of improving existing operations. It is also an intermittent process; it does not happen all the time (as the balancing process does). It happens only when a new threat or a new opportunity arises.

Through the combination of these three loops, a real-time organization senses and responds to change in a way that is both efficient and effective. Responsiveness happens when these three processes or feedback loops work simultaneously. Together, they produce a swarming dynamic that enables an organization to navigate through its environment and continuously adjust as the environment changes.[3]

Characteristics of the Responsive Organization

A central characteristic of responsive organizations is that they focus on analyzing and responding mostly to what can be called nonstandard input. This is because the real-time global economy is awash in data. It used to be only financial markets (stocks, commodities, futures) that generated this much data. Now everything generates continuous and growing streams of data. Cars, planes, and trains generate data from their onboard computers; companies generate data from their internal application networks; satellites beam down data from orbit; and the Internet moves all this data from anywhere to anywhere.

Companies are like fish swimming in an ocean of data. There is simply not time for people to handle or review standard information that just records the predictable, expected operations occurring in a company. Routine, standard data and procedures for handling it must be driven by automated transaction systems that support the company's standard operating procedures. Computers handle routine situations much better than humans because they never get bored by the routine, and they scale up quickly as transaction volumes increase.

People in a responsive organization need to devote their time to handling nonstandard data. Nonstandard data is any kind of data that is different from what is expected: data that for any reason does not conform to the rules built into automated transaction systems and performance parameters set in business monitoring systems. When a company's systems encounter this kind of data, people become involved. The greatest opportunities for any organization lie in the way they detect and respond to unexpected problems or threats or opportunities.

Nonstandard data triggers alerts that are sent to predefined groups of people involved in Loop 1 awareness activities. They analyze the nonstandard data and decide on the best response. If the best response involves fixing or improving an existing procedure or product, then a Loop 2 balancing process is initiated. If the best response involves creating a new process or product, then people initiate a Loop 3 agility process.

It is also import to understand that the effect of these three loops is to continuously change the organization's standard business process over time. A company's standard operating processes (SOPs) are not static; they are not bureaucratic activities tied up in red tape. Loop 2 is constantly adjusting and evolving existing procedures; and when Loop 3 creates new processes that work and deliver business success, then those new processes are added to or used to replace existing SOPs. So, in this way, the structure of the organization itself evolves and adapts to its changing environment.

Two Kinds of Responsiveness

In business, there are two kinds of responsiveness. The first kind is the one we think of most often; it's the rapid movement we call agility that companies use to create new products or procedures in response to emerging threats or opportunities. That kind of responsiveness is symbolized by a leaping panther going after its prey.

The agile response is called for when a company needs to act quickly and do something it has not done before. It requires the kind of concentration and focus that we see in panthers. You can see their eyes lock onto their target as soon as they discover it. You see them size up the situation and move with deliberate purpose into a position where they are best able to respond.

Then, at the right moment, panthers leap. It's a panther's agility that enables it to seize its prey or attack its enemy. Agility happens in quick sequences of moves; one move flows into the next, and it results in the panther's success. We'll talk more about this kind of agile responsiveness in the next two chapters.

The second kind of responsiveness is a slow and continuous adjustment to change in a company's environment. When done effectively, it produces steady and predictable flows of benefits. This is actually the more common type of responsiveness. It's a steady stream of small adjustments that people do so as to keep operations in balance as conditions change. That's the responsiveness symbolized by the sunflower. Since this is the most common kind of responsiveness, let's look at it here in a bit more detail.

Responsive Like a Sunflower

The sunflower is a very responsive plant. Between the time it first emerges from its seed until it flowers, its head and leaves follow the movement of the sun across the sky. A sunflower faces east in the morning and tracks the sun during the day, so that by the end of the day it faces west; then it starts all over again the next day. This movement allows the sunflower to maximize its interception of sunlight and optimizes exposure of its flower bud to sunlight as conditions change.

Sunflower responsiveness is analogous to the responsiveness that enables a company to increase productivity of its existing operations. (Photosynthesis is an existing operation in a sunflower.) Most activities in any company are related to carrying out SOPs, so there are a lot more opportunities to exercise this kind of agility than there are to exercise the other kind of responsiveness related to creating new products or services.

The responsiveness involved in constantly optimizing productivity of existing operations is guided by the action of balancing feedback loops. Balancing feedback loops seek to constantly make small adjustments in a system as its operating environment changes so that the system keeps functioning at an optimum level. In an organization, the trick is to identify the relevant balancing feedback loops at work and find ways to use them to drive operations in such a way as to keep productivity at the highest levels possible as situations change. Let me use a few analogies from the sunflower to illustrate what I mean.

Internal operations in a sunflower (or any other plant) are guided by the interaction of basic feedback loops. These feedback loops are driven by powerful forces in the sunflower's environment, such as sunlight, gravity, physical objects, and water. The feedback loops plants use to guide their internal operations are known as tropisms—that's the name given to the way a plant responds when it encounters one or more of these forces.

Four well-known plant tropisms are: (1) phototropism for responding to sunlight, (2) gravitropism for responding to gravity, (3) thigmotropism for responding to physical objects, and (4) hydrotropism for responding to water. All plants have differing capabilities in their operations that drive these four tropisms.

Sunflowers have taken phototropism to a new level and evolved a tropism called heliotropism that allows them to be even more responsive to sunlight. Heliotropic plants like sunflowers move their flowers and leaves in response to the sun so they track the sun's motion across the sky during the day. Through continuous small adjustments they receive a stream of small benefits that add up over time (like compound interest).[4]

The feedback loop that drives a sunflower's phototropism seems to be pretty simple. It's driven by a hormone that stimulates cell growth and cell enlargement wherever it is located. This hormone moves easily between the sunflower's cells, and it always moves away from sunlight. At night it's spread evenly throughout the plant; then with the sunrise, the hormone moves to the cells on the shaded west side of the plant. This causes those cells to enlarge so the stem bends to the east; as the sun moves during the day, the hormone continues migrating to the shaded part of the plant. By evening it's concentrated in cells on the east side of the plant so the stem is bending toward the setting sun in the west.

What happens if we apply this analogy of sunflower responsiveness to business? What tropisms might be (or could be) guiding the daily operations of a company, and what simple feedback loops might drive those operations? Is there a revenue-tropism somewhat like phototropism? Is there a profit-tropism somewhat like gravitropism? Is there a tropism that helps a company respond to changes in the cost of raw materials or health care?

STRUCTURE OF THE RESPONSIVE ORGANIZATION

The responsive organization is a network of autonomous operating units that employs the three process loops to create awareness, balance, and agility and uses this ability to thrive in its chosen environment. These networks can take many forms, and they can also be hybrid organizations that employ a mix of network structures in some areas and hierarchical structures in other areas. Operational decision-making authority is pushed out to autonomous operating units because that is the only way to act quickly enough to capitalize on opportunities and respond to threats in a timely manner.

Hierarchies worked well enough in the slower, more predictable industrial economy, but they cannot respond quickly enough to cope with our global real-time economy. By their very nature, hierarchies create communication and decision bottlenecks at the top. In slower times, hierarchies could deliver economies of scale through the use of SOPs that were put in place and rarely changed thereafter. But in the real-time economy, hierarchies cannot (because of their built-in bottlenecks) change operating procedures fast enough to keep up with the pace of change.

The reason networks work better than hierarchies in high-change and unpredictable environments is because, by their very nature, networks have built-in redundancy that provides them with the flexibility needed to make local decisions and respond quickly. In the slower industrial economy, this redundancy was seen as waste or unnecessary expense because organizations did not need to be flexible. For this reason, networks were regarded as less efficient than hierarchies.

That has changed. Flexibility is now critical to success. The autonomous operating units that make up a network have some duplication of people and functions, but that duplication gives them the capability to act on their own (autonomously), which is the source of a network's flexibility. Operating units act on their own to deal with some problems and collaborate with other operating units in the network when they need to handle other problems. Effective coordination happens in the network because all the operating units are self-motivated and their actions are guided by the rewards they gain by achieving certain agreed-upon objectives.

This is how responsive organizations come into being.

NOTES

1. An insightful discussion of the application of network organization structures to create responsive organizations is provided in a book written by Sally Helgesen, *The Web of Inclusion: A New Architecture for Building Great Organizations* (New York: Currency/Doubleday, 1995); see Chapter 2 "What It Is, How It Works, How It Feels," and Chapter 8 "The Hearth, the Hub, and the Working Club."

2. A thought-provoking exploration of the possibilities inherent in organizations that employ an implicit leadership model can be found in a book authored by Ori Brafman and Rod Backstrom, *The Starfish and the Spider: The Unstoppable Power of Leaderless Organizations* (New York: Penguin/Portfolio, 2006).

3. In my thinking about the way a responsive organization is structured, how it operates, and how it comes into being, I am much influenced by two books. One is by Kevin Kelly, *Out of Control: The New Biology of Machines, Social Systems and the Economic World* (New York: Addison-Wesley, 1995). The other is by Peter Senge, *The Fifth Discipline: The Art and Practice of the Learning Organization* (New York: Doubleday Business, 1994).

4. The basic plant tropisms are well explained and illustrated at a web site maintained by the University of Indiana named "Plants-In-Motion." The link to this site is: http://plantsinmotion.bio.indiana.edu/plantmotion/starthere.html. Further information about sunflowers and heliotropism can be found in the Wikipedia web site entry at: http://en.wikipedia.org/wiki/Sunflower (dated 24 November 2008).

CHAPTER 4

Speed, Simplicity, and Boldness

B usiness is certainly not war; business is about creation whereas war
is about destruction. Business happens when we find constructive
ways to meet our needs; war happens when we do not. Yet there
are useful analogies and lessons to be learned about responsiveness and
agility from military experience.

Sometimes people in the military are forced to learn lessons faster
than people in business because the consequences of failure in combat are
so severe. And military organizations all over the world have learned that
strategies and tactics emphasizing the use of responsiveness and agility
deliver the best results at the lowest cost in casualties and destruction.
In this chapter we will take a look at some of the approaches they have
found to be effective in situations analogous to situations that businesses
encounter.

FIVE THEMES FROM *THE ART OF WAR*

In any discussion of military strategy, one book in particular often comes up as a source for concepts and ideas. This book, written in China about 2,500 years ago by a Taoist philosopher named Sun Tzu, is called *The Art of War*.[1] It is not so much a book about war as it is a book about the art of competition and collaboration—whether in business, politics, the military, or even sports. This book has become required reading in the officer training programs of many of the world's military organizations (and it can also be found on reading lists at many fine business schools).

Sun Tzu's book embodies a spirit and approach to warfare and business that emphasizes responsiveness and agility. I have selected five themes from the book that speak to issues of strategy and tactics.[2] For each of these themes, I quote a relevant statement from Sun Tzu and then provide a few comments to illustrate how these statements relate to business. The five themes are:

1. Win Without Fighting
2. Avoid Strength, Attack Weakness
3. Know Truth, Sow Deception
4. Organize for Speed, Build Momentum
5. Shape Your Opponent, Choose Your Battles

Win Without Fighting

. . . those who win every battle are not really skillful—those who render others' armies helpless without fighting are the best of all.[3]

In business we compete with each other for customers by offering attractive products at good prices. When companies differentiate themselves from their competitors and offer unique and desirable products at profitable prices, they capture a market that is profitable. When they get into a price war with each other simply by offering products similar to their competitors at lower prices, they destroy the markets they are trying to capture. Whoever wins after a lengthy price war will capture a market that has little profit left in it, so it will not be worth much.

Avoid Strength, Attack Weakness

> Military formation is like water—the form of water is to avoid the high and go to the low, the form of a military force is to avoid the full and attack the empty; the flow of water is determined by the earth, the victory of a military force is determined by the opponent.[4]

All too often companies attack each other head on. All too often they make the obvious moves. Because those moves are so obvious, they are also easier to prepare for and easier for competitors to fend off. This is what happens in price wars or when companies launch copycat me-too products and services. If a company instead finds an unexpected new way to attract customers or a way to disrupt a competitor's supply chain, those actions are far more likely to succeed. And those successes will happen faster and cost much less than a direct frontal attack on a competitor's entrenched market position.

Know Truth, Sow Deception

> ... it is said that if you know others and know yourself, you will not be imperiled in a hundred battles; if you do not know others but know yourself, you win one and lose one; if you do not know others and do not know yourself, you will be imperiled in every single battle.[5]

Companies do not take the time to collect information and truly understand their situation and that of their competitors. Because the business world is awash in data, we feel overwhelmed by it all. We filter or summarize it, or we simply don't bother. But in that process, we often miss important information that could improve our chances of success. There are also tremendous competitive advantages to be gained by deceiving opponents and causing them to believe in and act on one assumption while we move in a different direction to attack them at an advantageous and unexpected location. Avoid making obvious and predictable moves.

Organize for Speed, Build Momentum

> Order and disorder are a matter of organization, courage and cowardice are a matter of momentum, strength and weakness are a matter of formation.[6]

The energy and commitment needed within a company to maintain speed and momentum require that the company be well organized and that its people enjoy the positive effects and rewards that this momentum can provide them. Once an advantage is perceived, companies must move quickly to capitalize on it. Once an advantage is gained, companies must keep moving to capitalize on new opportunities that appear. When companies pause, when they fail to follow up on opportunities in a timely manner, they lose their business advantage as competitors catch up with them.

Shape Your Opponent, Choose Your Battles

> ... those who skillfully move opponents make formations that opponents are sure to follow, give what opponents are sure to take. They move opponents with the prospect of gain, waiting for them in ambush.[7]

You can get competitors to react by offering something they want or threaten something they value; then they feel compelled to come to you. When you do this, you are setting the pace or tempo of the action and shaping the moves your opposition is likely to make; they begin to conform to your strategy instead of you conforming to theirs. If your company wants to invade a competitor's market; if you want to introduce a product that will attract your competitor's customers, then do things that get the competitor to respond in ways that work to your advantage. Wear away at your competitor's frame of mind and make it work hard to defend what it has. Avoid direct attacks and select targeted subgroups of their market to woo and win one by one.

INSIGHTS FROM PEOPLE WHO HAVE BEEN THERE

We continue this discussion of lessons that responsive businesses can learn from military experience with a few more insights from some influential practitioners. The first person is Liddell Hart, who wrote about and advocated a form of mobile warfare that was ignored by most militaries before World War II, but the German General Staff acknowledged his theories as a foundation of their Blitzkrieg tactics. The second person is General Erwin Rommel, and the third person is General George Patton.

Liddell Hart

Liddell Hart was a captain in the British Army and fought on the Western Front in Europe during World War I. He left the army in 1927 and spent the rest of his life as a writer, military correspondent, and strategist. He wrote some 30 books on military history and strategy from the 1930s up to his death in 1970. Perhaps his most useful book for businesspeople is a book titled simply *Strategy*[8] in which Hart investigates lessons learned from military operations starting with the Greeks in 490 BCE up through the first Arab-Israeli War of 1948.

In this book, Hart articulates a strategy he calls the "indirect approach" by which he means an approach to battle that involves doing the unexpected, using surprise, and avoiding the obvious, head-on, direct approach to battle. In his study of history, Hart notes that warfare is filled with examples of the direct approach, but that approach almost never produces a decisive result; instead, it results in battles of attrition that create great destruction and death and gain very little for either side. Here are several of Hart's thoughts on this subject.

> . . . the indirect approach is by far the most hopeful and economic form of strategy.[9]

> . . . history shows that rather than resign himself to a direct approach, a Great Captain will take even the most hazardous indirect approach—if necessary over mountains, deserts or swamps, with only a fraction of his

force, even cutting himself loose from his communications. He prefers to face any unfavorable condition rather than accept the risk of frustration inherent in the direct approach.[10]

The most effective indirect approach is one that lures or startles the opponent into a false move—so that, as in ju-jitsu, his own effort is turned into the lever of his overthrow.[11]

Whatever the form, the effect to be sought is the dislocation of the opponent's mind and dispositions—such an effect is the true gauge of an indirect approach.[12]

... in the face of the overwhelming evidence of history, no general is justified in launching his troops in a direct attack upon an enemy firmly in position ... instead of seeking to upset the enemy's equilibrium by one's attack, it must be upset before a real attack is, or can be successfully launched.[13]

... the unexpected cannot guarantee success. But it guarantees the best chance of success.[14]

Erwin Rommel

Erwin Rommel served in the German Army during both world wars and published a book titled *Infantry Attacks*[15] before the start of World War II. It describes mobile infantry tactics he developed during the first world war that used surprise and combinations of different weapons to attack and defeat opponents. From his campaigns in North Africa during World War II, General Rommel, became known as the "Desert Fox." He compiled voluminous notes containing battle maps, snapshots, letters to his wife, and thoughts on his strategy and tactics and those of his opponents. In the fall of 1944, he was implicated in a plot to assassinate Hitler, and the Gestapo ordered him to commit suicide. After the war Rommel's wife asked Liddell Hart to edit his memoirs, and they were published in a book titled *The Rommel Papers*.[16] A few of Rommel's insights are quoted next.

It is often possible to decide the issue of a battle merely by making an unexpected shift of one's main weight.[17]

The enemy's plan had been extremely simple, but simple plans are in most cases more menacing than complex ones.[18]

Their unwieldy and rigidly methodical technique of command, their over-systematic issuing of orders down to the last detail, leaving little latitude to the junior commander, and their poor adaptability to the changing course of the battle were also much to blame for the British failures.[19]

The main endeavor should be to concentrate one's own forces in space and time, while at the same time seeking to split the enemy forces spatially and destroy them at different times.[20]

It is my experience that bold decisions give the best promise of success. But one must differentiate between strategic or tactical boldness and a military gamble. A bold operation is one in which success is not a certainty but which in case of failure leaves one with sufficient forces in hand to cope with whatever situation may arise. A gamble, on the other hand, is an operation which can lead either to victory or to the complete destruction of one's force.[21]

George S. Patton

George Patton was a commander in the new U.S. Army Tank Corps in World War I, and during World War II he was one of the most effective Allied generals in combining armored units, artillery, infantry, and air support to win battles and conduct sweeping campaigns. He read the works of both Liddell Hart and Rommel and put their ideas to use. He fought in North Africa, Sicily, and Europe and died in 1945, soon after the end of the war. His wife edited his papers and notes and published his memoirs in a book titled *War as I Knew It*.[22] Patton is known for his pithy comments; some of them are quoted next.

A good plan, violently executed now, is better than a perfect plan next week.[23]

Don't tell people how to do things, tell them what to do and let them surprise you with their results.[24]

If you tell people where to go, but not how to get there, you'll be amazed at the results.[25]

Success in war depends on the golden rules of war: speed, simplicity, and boldness.[26]

OBSERVE—ORIENT—DECIDE—ACT

One of the most influential military thinkers since World War II was Colonel John Boyd. He was a jet fighter pilot who fought in the Korean War, and after the war he became an instructor at the U.S. Air Force's Fighter Weapons School. When Boyd researched the results of aerial combat from the Korean War, he noticed it was not the biggest or fastest aircraft that won dogfights. Instead, it was the most maneuverable aircraft flown by pilots who knew how to use rapid sequences of maneuvers to confuse and defeat their opponents.[27]

These findings squared with Boyd's own experience, and he pursued a lifelong journey of study and teaching. He read the books and reports of hundreds of military practitioners and theorists and was at the center of a lively group at the Pentagon that debated and formulated a controversial body of military theories in the 1980s. Boyd's theories are now used by military organizations around the world.

Boyd articulated what he learned about the best way to deal with fast-paced and complex environments and encapsulated his teachings in a learnable and repeatable process that shows individuals and whole organizations how to compete and win in any high-change situation. He named this process "Observe—Orient—Decide—Act" (OODA)—also known as the OODA Loop or Boyd Cycle.[28]

Following the Four Steps

There are four steps in the OODA Loop. The first step is to *Observe*. This is the process of collecting and communicating information about the environment. The next step is to *Orient*. This is the most important activity because it is where information is turned into an understanding of the situation upon which the next two steps will depend. In this step, the environment is described, the positions of the different players in the environment are defined, and the relevant trends, threats, and opportunities are identified. In the *Decide* step, different responses and plans for implementing them are created and evaluated. The most appropriate response is chosen, and that leads to the final step: *Act*. In this step, action is taken and results occur that are either favorable, not favorable, or indeterminate. These results are picked up in the Observe step and the loop continues.

It is important to note that the OODA Loop does not require people or organizations to cycle through all four steps all of the time. It is not a lockstep sequence. When an environment is well understood, the Decide step is not needed. You can cycle quickly between Observe, Orient, and Act in a series of rapid responses. At other times you may decide not to Act at all and just Observe and Orient, waiting for an appropriate opportunity to Act. It is better to think of the OODA Loop as an interactive network of activities with the Orient step at its core instead of a fixed series of steps. The OODA Loop is what happens in the first of the three main feedback loops (Loop 1—Awareness) that drive a responsive organization (see Chapter 5). The OODA Loop is illustrated in Figure 4.1.

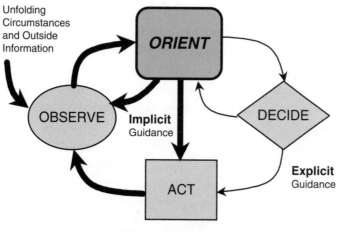

FIGURE 4.1   The OODA Loop

Those players who learn to shorten the time needed to Observe, Orient, Decide, and Act are the ones who can set the pace and tempo of events. They seize the initiative, and all the other players wind up reacting to their moves. It is not the absolute speed of the cycle that matters but your speed relative to your competitors.

The Most Important Step: Orient

Let's take a closer look at the Orient step because it is the most important one. People form a picture of their world in the Orient step, and this picture of the world drives their decisions and actions that follow. Good orientation is central to your ability to take effective action and achieve desirable results.

The Orient step needs the most support from business intelligence and related systems capabilities. The real world unfolds in "an irregular, disorderly, unpredictable manner," as John Boyd put it. Responsive organizations watch their business environments and make decisions about how best to respond as day-to-day and week-to-week situations unfold. Boyd taught that effective competitors in any environment constantly look for mismatches between their initial understanding of the environment and new circumstances as they unfold. In those mismatches there are often opportunities for a competitor to seize new advantages.

Another major concept of the OODA Loop implies that everyone in an agile organization has a common understanding of the organization's purpose and its current objectives. In military organizations this is known as the commander's intent and the mission orders—people are told what needs to be done, but they are not told how to do it. They are not micromanaged; instead they are trained and trusted to assess situations in the light of their commander's intent and do the right thing to accomplish their mission.

The OODA Loop expresses this understanding of the commander's intent with the notions of implicit guidance and explicit guidance. (See the section "Leadership for the Responsive Organization" in Chapter 3.) When the people in a company have clear performance objectives and know what management expects of them and when they possess accurate, timely information about their own performance, they take their own corrective actions as demanded by the situation. As shown by the heavier lines on the OODA Loop diagram, responsive companies use implicit guidance most of the time because it allows them to operate more quickly.

Company executives provide explicit guidance when they make decisions to change strategy and stop or start projects. Executives use explicit guidance when the rules of the game change. When this happens, people need to be informed of the changes and told how those changes affect their jobs and performance expectations. Then people can readjust, and implicit guidance again takes over to guide their actions.

Boyd borrowed heavily from Sun Tzu and incorporated his teachings on the use of orthodox and unorthodox responses—*cheng* and *ch'i*—to master a situation. It is a mixture of the traditional and the unexpected that produces the best results. Traditional, orthodox responses can be performed very rapidly to counter or exploit certain events. Unexpected, unorthodox responses serve to disorient competitors and cause them to pause, to question, and to wonder what will happen next. This slows down and stretches out competitors' OODA Loop cycle time.

MANEUVER WARFARE

The principles defined by Sun Tzu, Liddell Hart, John Boyd, and others have led to the formation of a body of theory and practice known as maneuver warfare. Maneuver warfare is based on concepts of responsiveness and agility. It draws heavily on strategy and tactics demonstrated by military practitioners, such as certain German and Allied commanders during World War II and the practices of military organizations such as the U.S. Marine Corps, the Israel Defense Forces, and rapid-reaction forces of countries around the world.[29]

Maneuver warfare aims to win wars quickly and with less destruction than would be incurred by more conventional warfare, where enemies attack one another head on and engage in prolonged wars of attrition. It places an emphasis on confusing the opponent by sudden, unexpected movements. Practitioners of maneuver warfare seek to demoralize their opponents by consistently cycling through their OODA Loops faster than their opponents.

Those who can cycle through the process faster than their competition start to realize an ever-increasing advantage with each cycle. Slower competitors fall farther and farther behind and become less and less able to cope with their deteriorating situations. With each OODA Loop cycle, the actions of the slower competitors become less and less relevant or appropriate to the actual circumstances, leading to their final collapse.

Practitioners of maneuver warfare accept confusion and disorder and learn to operate successfully within such situations. To do this, they organize themselves into networks of highly autonomous operating units that coordinate their actions using the concepts of commander's intent and mission orders. They do this because only decentralized networks of operating units with local authority to act can move quickly enough to succeed in maneuver warfare. If units have to pass observations up the chain of command and wait for orders to come back down before they act, then their OODA Loop cycles will be way too slow. What does this say about how a responsive business should be organized?

In addition to supporting the commander's intent and the use of mission orders, maneuver warfare is guided by several other key concepts. Two of the most important ones that have direct relevance to business are the concepts of *Schwerpunkt* and combined arms.

Schwerpunkt—The Focus of Effort

The German generals in World War II who commanded mobile armored forces developed a body of concepts and tactics known as Blitzkrieg. One of the most important of these is a concept known as *Schwerpunkt* which means the center of gravity or the focus point. It means you focus your effort to strike hard against one of the enemy's weak points. After assessing the situation and the terrain, the *Schwerpunkt* is where you determine you can do something to deliver decisive results and win the battle.

The *Schwerpunkt* is both a physical point of main attack and also a conceptual point. The *Schwerpunkt* is chosen so that it harmonizes both the commander's intent and the mission orders given to various combat units involved in a battle. It pulls together the efforts of all subordinates and guides them toward achieving the result their commander wants.

Instead of trying to do 10 different things, people focus on doing one important thing. This calls for intelligence, clarity of purpose, and courage on the part of the commander. A common mistake is trying to cover all the bases; that is a symptom of an inability to make decisions.[30]

Combined Arms

Maneuver warfare calls for the use of combined arms to increase striking power. Combined arms is a technique where people use combinations of weapons so that opponents are attacked with two or more arms simultaneously, and any action opponents take to defend themselves from one type of attack makes them vulnerable to attack from the other weapons. It places opponents on the horns of a dilemma and weakens their will to resist. Maneuver warfare units use teams of people who fight with different weapons and closely coordinate their actions with each other to achieve a powerful overall effect that is greater than what any one weapon alone could deliver.[31]

Here is an example. By combining the use of three relatively simple weapons—land mines, machine guns, and mortars—a formidable barrier can quickly be created to stop the advance of opposing troops. The combination of these weapons creates an effect that is more powerful than what any one weapon could deliver on its own. It works like this: Advancing soldiers encounter the land mines so they slow down to look for mines. But by going slow, they become easy targets for the machine guns and they risk setting off mines if they dive for cover. Then, as they realize their predicament and turn to escape, they are cut down by the mortar shells that start falling in their midst. The effect of combining these three weapons is to trap, demoralize, and then destroy advancing troops.

Does this paint a vivid picture of how to use combinations of different technologies in war to magnify the destructive effect? What can be learned from this example about how to create combinations of different technologies in business to magnify the productive and creative effect?

We need to get over any illusions that one piece of technology or one business activity all by itself is going to solve the problems a business may have. The principle of combined arms teaches us beyond any doubt that we must use combinations of technologies and tactics to deal with situations. We need to employ technologies where each is used for its strengths and is combined with other technologies with complementary strengths. This is the way to generate a tremendous multiplier effect.

What would happen if people at different levels of an organization used information systems that showed them an integrated picture of what was happening hour by hour and day by day in the different areas of their organization? Suppose people in operations could see product inventory on hand in various locations and daily product demand at these locations. Suppose people in marketing and sales could see sales trends for the company's products and could see customer response rates for various advertising and promotional campaigns. Suppose people in finance could see the company's daily operating expenses and its bank account balances and amounts of money being collected from customers each day.

What would happen if these information systems also alerted relevant people in the organization when data collected from certain operating areas indicated activities in those areas were starting to drift outside of predefined performance ranges? What if people could then access other systems that let them get more detailed information and quickly do research on performance patterns and trends in those areas? What if people could call up simulation models of current business operations and test out probable effects of changes in the tasks and workflows in those areas? What level of business performance would be enabled by combining these different information technologies and systems?

With proper training and motivation, do you think teams of people using combinations of technologies like these would become very skilled at doing their jobs? Do you think they could use these technologies to grow and maintain very effective and profitable businesses? We will look at this idea in greater depth in Chapter 6.

MODERN WARFIGHTING

The U.S. Marine Corps is certainly the very model of a thoroughly modern mobile military; and the fact that it has adopted maneuver warfare as its combat doctrine speaks volumes about what the future of warfare will look like. Much of this doctrine is encapsulated in a short handbook titled *Warfighting*.[32] Every Marine, from new recruits to the Commandant of the Corps, is expected to read it and understand it and apply its principles.

What follows are a few excerpts from this book that have particular relevance to businesses that are trying to become more responsive and more agile. The meaning of these excerpts is clear and their implications for business operating models are self-evident. (Italics are in the original text.)

> By historical standards, the modern battlefield is particularly disorderly. While past battlefields could be described by linear formations and uninterrupted linear fronts, we cannot think of today's battlefield in linear terms.[33]

> By definition, maneuver relies on speed and surprise, for without either we cannot concentrate strength against enemy weakness . . . maneuver incompetently applied carries with it a greater chance for catastrophic failure, while attrition is inherently less risky.[34]

> Purposely choosing the more difficult course because it is less expected necessarily means sacrificing efficiency to some degree.[35]

> By exploiting opportunities, we create in increasing numbers more opportunities for exploitation. It is often the ability and the willingness to ruthlessly exploit these opportunities that generate decisive results.[36]

> *Equipment that permits overcontrol of units in battle is in conflict with the Marine Corps' philosophy of command and is not justifiable.*[37]

> In order to minimize research and development costs and fielding time, the Marine Corps will exploit existing capabilities—"off-the-shelf" technology—to the greatest extent possible.[38]

First and foremost, *in order to generate the tempo of operations we desire and to best cope with the uncertainty, disorder, and fluidity of combat, command must be decentralized.* That is, subordinate commanders must make decisions on their own initiative, based on their understanding of the senior's intent, rather than passing information up the chain of command and waiting for the decision to be passed down.[39]

Our philosophy must not only accommodate but exploit human traits such as boldness, initiative, personality, strength of will, and imagination.[40]

Case Study: The Tao of Supply Chains

Here is a real story about applying the concepts and practices described in this chapter to drive responsiveness and agility and deliver tangible value measured in real dollars. It illustrates the application of concepts such as commander's intent, defining the focus of effort, and use of off-the-shelf technology as well as orthodox and unorthodox approaches.[41] It is also a story of how information technology (IT) can be used to enable this success.

In 2004 I was chief information officer (CIO) of a national distribution organization (Network Services Company) providing customers with food service disposables, janitorial supplies, and printing paper. The organization was owned by its 76 member companies, and each had its own facilities and internal IT systems. Each company had its own local customers and we worked together to serve national account customers.

Members' collective revenue was over $8 billion, and Network's total national account revenue was over $550 million and growing by double-digit percentages every year. We provided customers with a tailored package of products and supply chain services to support their business and lower their overall operating costs.

One of our biggest national account customers was a chain of stores that each holiday season used specially printed paper items to promote its holiday theme. Those items were used in the customer's 4,500 restaurants during November and December. At the end of January, remaining inventory had to be written off. The same holiday print designs were never used two years in a row. In years past, there had been excess inventory of around 4 percent, amounting to almost $600,000 in costs that had to be written off by the customer.

This customer hired a new purchasing manager who decided we could all do better than that. He called us out to the company's headquarters that summer for a meeting, and he announced his intention (here is the commander's intent) to reduce excess inventory of the specially printed holiday items by 50 percent or more. We still had to maintain 100 percent product availability for all its stores and minimize expensive movements of inventory from one region to another to meet unexpected demand. He asked us how we were going to work with him to make that happen. I told him we understood what he wanted and that we'd be back in touch with the specifics in a few weeks.

As we flew home, our sales director on the account told me this was a high-visibility project with the customer, and we had to figure out how to do it. He reminded me that it was already halfway through the summer, so we had to be ready to go in 90 days because we would begin stocking inventory in our distribution centers by October. And, of course, we couldn't spend lots of money on this because margins were tight. In addition, all the parties in this supply chain used different enterprise resource planning (ERP) systems. And even within Network, the 26 member companies that served the account used different ERP systems. Several times on that flight, I experienced a sudden falling sensation in my stomach, and it wasn't due to air turbulence.

Times like these test my skill and self-confidence; my reputation for responding fast and effectively to business needs hangs in the balance. Can I rise to the challenge, or will I flee in panic? For me, the answer lies in doing three things: First, take a deep breath; second, take another deep breath; and third, remember *The Art of War* and ask, "What would Master Sun do?"

One of the lessons I've been able to absorb from Master Sun tells me that apparent complexity is really composed of simple underlying patterns. If I can discern those underlying patterns, then I can devise simple and effective responses. So what was the pattern here? As I saw it, the need was to track daily product usage, constantly update demand forecasts, move inventory so as to cover demands, and use it all up by the end of the season.

That meant effective collaboration among all parties in the supply chain to respond as actual demand unfolded. If our initial assumptions about demand were not entirely accurate (and they never are), we needed to be able to reposition inventory among distribution centers earlier and more efficiently without sudden costly air-freighting of paper goods to stores across the country. (These are the mission orders.)[42]

(continued)

So, I asked myself, "What can IT provide that will enable this collaboration?" Obviously, what was needed was a continually updated, end-to-end view of product in the supply chain that was visible at all times to people at my company, the manufacturers, and the customer. That would be the basis for our collaboration and decision making (here is the focus of effort—*Schwerpunkt*).

I knew of several fine software vendors' products that could do that, but they cost more money than I had to spend and took more time to install than I had available. So much for the orthodox ideas. What else could I do? Master Sun says, ". . . those skilled at the unorthodox are infinite as heaven and earth, inexhaustible as the great rivers." Wow. What unorthodox ideas could I come up with?

Master Sun says, "There are only five notes in the musical scale, but their variations are so many that they cannot all be heard. There are only five basic colors, but their variations are so many that they cannot all be seen." Does this mean that there is a combination of basic IT components that I could use to quickly create my end-to-end supply chain picture and keep it constantly updated?

What basic IT components do all parties in this supply chain have easy access to (use of off-the-shelf technology to minimize development costs and fielding time), and how could I combine them into the system I needed? I'm not going to give you the whole answer right now because then you wouldn't get to practice your own agility and figure it out for yourself. But I will give you some hints. The components are spreadsheets, text files, e-mail, a few Web pages, a relational database, and some small programs that took about three weeks to write and test. (You can contact me at my Web site: www.michaelhugos.com. I'll be glad to share the details with you.)

We assembled these components (analogous to combined arms) into a system that collected data from all members of the supply chain and displayed it in easily defined and formatted numeric and graphic reports. The data consisted of inventory amounts that were in production, in warehouses, and on order. It also included invoice data that showed our deliveries to the customer's stores, which allowed us to track actual demand at the store levels and regional levels.

The system was up and running by October. It was extremely cost-effective to build (use of speed, simplicity, and boldness). We used it to facilitate weekly conference calls that increased in frequency as the season progressed. On those calls, we all reviewed the numbers and projected run-out dates. We made decisions and continued to tweak the system to incorporate new views of the data and new calculations.

We reduced excess inventory from 4 percent in prior years to 1.3 percent that year on increased total sales, and the dollar value of the excess inventory dropped to less than $200,000. As we reviewed the holiday season results in January, the new purchasing manager said he was quite pleased with our performance. And then we started a new project to work with him and the manufacturers to document what we learned, make further improvements, and extend the system to cover the rollout of other new products—not just holiday items ("By exploiting opportunities, we create in increasing numbers more opportunities for exploitation.").

Thank you, Master Sun.

NOTES

1. Sun Tzu, *The Art of War*, trans. Thomas Cleary, (Boston: Shambhala Publications, 1988). There are many different translations of this classic book; this edition is my favorite.
2. There are also many commentaries on how to apply concepts in *The Art of War* to both military and business operations. A thoughtful commentary in this area is written by a former U.S. Army officer who is now a business strategist; his name is Mark McNeilly, and his book is *Sun Tzu and the Art of Business* (New York: Oxford University Press, 2000). I am much influenced by the six strategic principles that Mr. McNeilly has identified from Sun Tzu's teaching.
3. Sun Tzu, *The Art of War*, 67.
4. Ibid., 112.
5. Ibid., 82.
6. Ibid., 97.
7. Ibid., 101.
8. B.H. Liddell Hart, *Strategy*, 2nd rev. ed. (New York: Plume/Penguin Group, 1991).
9. Ibid., 145.
10. Ibid., 146.
11. Ibid., 146.
12. Ibid., 147.
13. Ibid., 147.
14. Ibid., 337.
15. Erwin Rommel, *Infantry Attacks* (Mechanicsburg, PA: Stackpole Books, 1995).
16. Erwin Rommel, *The Rommel Papers*, ed. B. H. Liddell Hart (Cambridge, MA: Da Capo Press, 1982).
17. Ibid., 144.
18. Ibid., 147.

19. Ibid., 184.

20. Ibid., 199.

21. Ibid., 201.

22. George S. Patton, *War as I Knew It,* ed. Beatrice Patton (New York: Pyramid Books/Houghton Mifflin, 1966).

23. Ibid., 354.

24. This quote from George S. Patton can be found on Famous Quotes at: http://www.famous-quotes.net/Author.aspx?George_Patton.

25. This quote from George S. Patton can be found on ThinkExist at: http://thinkexist.com/quotation/if_you_tell_people_where_to_go-but_not_how_to_get/207386.html.

26. This quote from George S. Patton can be found on the Patton Society Web site at: http://www.pattonhq.com/unknown/chap13.html.

27. Robert Coram, *Boyd: The Fighter Pilot Who Changed the Art of War* (New York: Little Brown and Company, 2002). This book does a great job of describing Boyd's life and work.

28. Material on the OODA Loop can be found in Robert Coram's book and on the Internet at several Web sites. Two authoritative Web sites are www.belisarius.com and www.d-n-i.net.

29. A definitive work on maneuver warfare is by William Lind: *Maneuver Warfare Handbook* (Boulder, CO: Westview Press, 1985). The appendix to the book consists of a series of lectures delivered by Colonel Michael Wyly, USMC (Ret.) at the Amphibious Warfare School in 1981–1982; these lectures provide insightful examples of applying maneuver warfare concepts to the conduct of specific military operations and battles.

30. Ibid., 111.

31. Ibid., 113.

32. U.S. Marine Corps, *Warfighting* (New York: Currency/Doubleday, 1989).

33. Ibid., 11.

34. Ibid., 32.

35. Ibid., 43.

36. Ibid., 48.

37. Ibid., 68.

38. Ibid.

39. Ibid., 79.

40. Ibid., 80.

41. This case study was written by the author and first published as "The Tao of Supply Chains" in *CIO* magazine, Vol. 18/No. 15, pp. 38–40, 15 May 2005.

42. A concise discussion of ways to apply John Boyd's ideas and other maneuver war concepts to business is found in a book written by a former associate of Boyd, Chet Richards *Certain to Win: The Strategy of John Boyd Applied to Business* (Philadelphia, PA: Xlibris Corporation, 2004).

CHAPTER **5**

Strategically Focused, Tactically Responsive

U se the principles of the responsive organization to structure your company's operations; apply the lessons of speed, simplicity, and boldness to guide your actions; and what emerges is a business model that delivers alpha profits on a consistent basis. Let's explore this business model in a bit more depth. To do this we will use the three process loops presented in Chapter 3—Awareness, Balance, and Agility—to organize our discussion.

These three loops apply to running individual business units just as well as they apply to running a whole organization. I used the three feedback loops to run the information systems group of a multibillion-dollar distribution cooperative. We became the focused and responsive group that developed and operated the systems infrastructure that enabled our company to transform its business model from an old-line distributor to a value-added provider of products and supply chain services.

AWARENESS DRIVES EFFECTIVE STRATEGY (LOOP 1)

John Boyd described strategy as "a mental tapestry of changing intentions for harmonizing and focusing our efforts; as a basis for realizing some aim or purpose in an unfolding and often unforeseen world; of many bewildering events and many contending interests."[1]

The purpose of Loop 1 is to create that ever-changing mental tapestry and deliver business success. The four steps of the OODA Loop create an awareness of changing market conditions and internal operations. All good strategies come from an accurate appraisal of existing conditions and changes as they happen. OODA Loop activities are where senior executives can spend most of their time and deliver the greatest value to their organizations.

As a company's business environment evolves over time, executives use the OODA Loop to constantly assess changes and gauge the impact of these changes on the company. Executives need to ask themselves and ask their staff questions such as: Do existing company operations and organization structures support our new business strategies? What new capabilities are needed? How can we best leverage existing systems and operations? And what new systems are needed?

Executives need to know when business activities increase or decrease at unexpected rates or when system processing or operating errors occur at greater than expected rates. Events like these usually signify a need to improve some existing operation.

They also need to know when new competitors enter the market and when sales of certain products increase or decrease faster than expected. Events like these often signify a need to create new systems or new business operations.

For example, consider the response you would make to the unexpected news that sales of your company's new product X were increasing much faster than had been anticipated and also that customers who bought product X were two-thirds more likely then to purchase product Y within the following 60 days. The way you respond to this unexpected news and the speed with which your organization delivers needed support will be a big determining factor in how much success and profitability your company can achieve.

You need to consider the information systems and business operations that support product X and determine how to scale them up faster than originally planned in order to handle the extra sales volume. You also decide what new operations will enable the company to best exploit the emerging opportunity for sales of product Y and figure out how soon they need to be in place.

You might decide to launch two projects simultaneously. One project would accelerate the build-out of processing capacity for the systems that support product X and expand the customer service group that supports the product. This is a Loop 2 Balancing project because it is part of improving existing processes and systems; it will deliver more efficiency. Balancing means continuous improvement and fine tuning.

Your other project might be to develop new systems to address the emerging opportunity for product Y and other follow-on product sales. This is a Loop 3 Agility project. This will create a new process to deal with a new event; it will deliver effectiveness. Agility means move it or lose—respond quickly before the opportunity disappears.

BALANCING MEANS CONTINUOUS IMPROVEMENT (LOOP 2)

Six sigma is a process based on the techniques of total quality management developed by W. Edwards Deming and Toyota Motor Corporation in the 1960s and 1970s. In the 1980s Motorola expanded on these techniques and created a repeatable process for applying them to solve problems and improve quality. Now six sigma is widely used by organizations around the world.

The process provides guidance to organizations and project teams as they work through projects to improve their operations or their products. A five-step process guides project teams through their work:

1. Define.
2. Measure.
3. Analyze.

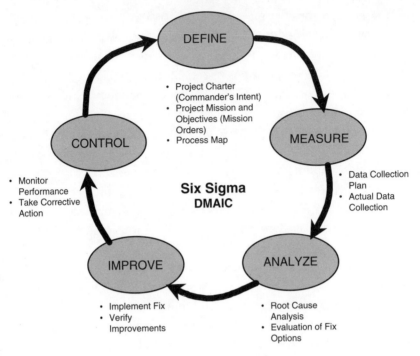

FIGURE 5.1   Loop 2: Balancing Process

4. Improve.

5. Control.[2]

The process is known as DMAIC (from first letter of each step) and is pronounced "dee-MAY-ic," Let's take a quick look at the activities in each step. Figure 5.1 maps out the process.

Define

The Define step begins a six sigma project and produces three important documents. The first document is the project charter. The charter lays out the business case and the problem statement. It also clearly defines the project scope so that the project team knows exactly where to focus and what they should avoid. (This is the commander's intent.) The charter also articulates the goal or mission of the project and the specific objectives that the team needs to achieve in order to accomplish the goal. (These are the mission orders for the team.)

In addition to the project charter, the second document produced in this step defines the customers that will be served and their needs and expectations. The needs and expectations of customers tell the team what activities to measure and improve. The third document is a high-level process map that shows the tasks involved in those activities and the inputs and outputs of each task. It shows everyone involved with the project the tasks that are candidates for improvement. The actual people who do the work in the activities or business operations that will be improved usually make up most of the project team members.

Measure

In this step the project team creates a data collection plan and then collects data that measures the current state of the operation or product targeted for improvement. The data collected reflects customer requirements and shows how often those requirements are actually met. The data also shows the frequency levels of key tasks in the process.

After collecting the data, the team calculates the existing sigma measurement for the operation. This step of collecting data and documenting the current situation is often overlooked or done poorly because the project team thinks they already know what is wrong and they want to get on to fixing the problem. Good data collection gets the project off to a start in the right direction.

Analyze

In this step the project team applies statistical analysis tools to discover and validate root causes of problems. Many of the tools used in this step come from total quality management. The team uses cause-and-effect diagrams and frequency distribution charts to pinpoint the sources of error in the process being investigated. They use scatter diagrams to test the strength of correlations between one variable and another in the operation. And they use run charts to track the performance patterns of various tasks and of the operation overall.

As they pinpoint problems, the team then formulates options for eliminating or reducing these problems and compares the different options. How difficult is each option? How much will each cost? What impact will each option have on improving the sigma measure of the operation?

Improve

In this step the team leader works with the project's executive sponsor to select a group of improvement options. They choose the options with the best chance for success and with the greatest impact.

With the sponsor's backing, the DMAIC team implements the selected improvement. Best practice calls for the team to implement the improvements one at a time or in small groups of related improvements. After implementing each improvement, the team should collect process performance data and recalculate the sigma measure; it is hoped that the sigma measure improves. Recollection and recalculation ensures that the improvements actually provide valuable results or they are discontinued.

Control

Once a project team makes process improvements to their workflow, they regularly monitor the process to assure that the improvements stay in place and remain effective. The project team defines a set of measurements that will be collected on an ongoing basis by appropriate systems to document the performance levels of the improved operation. The team also creates a response plan that lays out corrective actions to take if ongoing performance measures indicate that the improvements are beginning to slip.

Over the long term, the greatest benefit from the six sigma approach is that organizations reap the very real benefits of improvements that continue to deliver more and more value. These operating improvements enable the organization to flex and adjust as its environment changes so that the organization's operations remain responsive and operate efficiently.

It is very important to note that the control process is performed by the people who actually do the work, not by their supervisors. They are able to see continuous performance statistics as they do their work, and they respond so as to keep nudging their performance levels toward six sigma day after day as operating conditions change. These continuous adjustments produces results over time that are analogous to the effects of compound interest; it produces 2 to 4 percent extra productivity and profitability year after year.

This is also analogous to the way a sunflower regulates its operations so as to keep the face of the flower pointed toward the sun as the sun moves across the sky; the result is that the plant is able to maximize its photosynthesis each day. (See the discussion about this in Chapter 3.)

Constant Balancing and Fine-Tuning

One sigma means a business process met customer expectations 30.9 percent of the time. Two sigma means 69.1 percent, three sigma means 93.3 percent, four sigma means 99.4 percent, five sigma is 99.97 percent, and six sigma is 99.99966 percent. Most companies operate in the range between two and three sigma. A 93.32 percent customer satisfaction rate (3σ) is pretty good, but it means that there are still 66,807 failures per million events. That produces a lot of unhappy customers and a lot of unnecessary expenses.

Competitive advantage goes to those companies that can drive performance closest to six sigma and then *keep it there* as conditions change over time. This is obviously not easy. It requires a level of training and focus that most organizations do not yet posses. This is the responsiveness symbolized by the continuous adjustments of the sunflower (see Figure 5.2).

AGILITY MEANS MOVE IT OR LOSE (LOOP 3)

To paraphrase a famous quote from Thomas Edison, the agile and innovative use of business systems is 5 percent inspiration and 95 percent

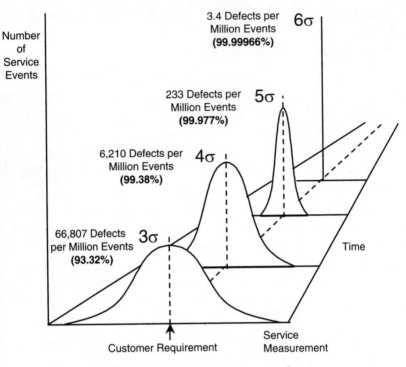

FIGURE 5.2   Six Sigma (6σ) Is Almost Perfect

perspiration. Let's talk about that 95 percent part. It means a lot more than just working hard. It means using a fast and flexible process to develop and deploy new systems and business operations.

That process has to enable agility by showing people how to move forward in quick, focused steps. Since all jobs expand to fill whatever time is available, an agile process requires you to set an appropriate time frame for getting things done and then shape the job so as to finish it within the time available. Agility means that you are faster than your competition. Agile time frames are measured in weeks and months, not years.

Business executives can also use agility to boost innovation. An innovative process calls for people to feel a sense of urgency in order to overcome the inertia of doing things the same old way. So placing limits on the time and money that your employees can spend to solve a problem is a great way to create urgency. I'm not talking about doing things on the cheap; I'm talking about doing them faster and smarter.

In the past, I have challenged my own staff to innovate solutions that cost 10 times less than what our competition is spending and that can be developed four times faster—what I call 10/4 performance.

Agility and innovation starts with a frame of mind, and that frame of mind is embodied in a three-step process I call Define-Design-Build. It's a simple, easily understood process that guides people through the three steps of developing any new system or business process.

Each step produces a well-defined set of deliverables and has tight time boxes and budget guidelines. See Figure 5.3 for a list of the deliverables, the time boxes, and budgets. Most important is the way that this process enables agility and innovation.

The Define step takes two to three weeks and costs 5 to 10 percent of the total project budget. The Design step takes one to three months and costs 15 to 30 percent of the total budget. The Build step takes two to six months and costs 60 to 80 percent of the total budget.

You may ask how I know these time frames without knowing the specifics of a given project. My answer is that there is only that much time available if you are truly going to be agile. If people can't define what is needed within two to six weeks, then it certainly won't be an agile

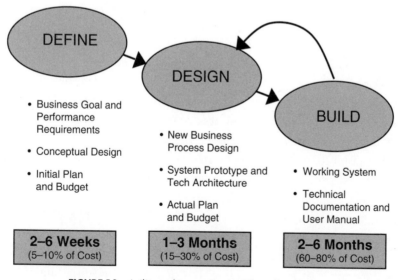

FIGURE 5.3   Agility and Innovation in a Three-Step Process

project. Likewise, I know the design work will cost only 15 to 30 percent of the total project budget because if people are spending more than that, they are designing something too complex. More expensive projects will take longer than one to three months to design and then will take too long to build. In sum, if the work cannot meet these requirements, then stop the project because whatever is being done is neither innovative nor agile.

Here are some other things I emphasize in the Define-Design-Build process. First of all, every project needs a full-time person in charge who has the skills and authority to get things done and is totally committed to success. I call that person the system builder. Without such a person, no project can succeed. Make sure you have good system builders for every project you start.

Next, build robust 80 percent solutions rather than attempting to build 100 percent solutions. Avoid the temptation to overengineer your systems in an attempt to handle every possible combination of events. Trying to build systems that can handle everything increases the cost and complexity in an exponential fashion. Have people, not computers, handle the exceptions and the one-off occurrences, and develop systems to handle only the routine, day-in, day-out transactions. This is how you build systems for 10 times less than your competition.

Remember that big systems are always composed of a collection of smaller subsystems. So once the Define step is completed, big, multimillion-dollar projects can be broken up into smaller projects to develop each subsystem. Instead of one big project team designing everything and then building everything, this arrangement allows multiple smaller teams to design and build subsystems in parallel, under the overall direction of the system builder. This is how to get things done four times faster than your competition.

At first people may accuse executives who adopt a process such as Define-Design-Build of being overly demanding and unreasonable. I admit my three steps have also been called "Move it! Move it! Move it!" But do not relent. What you ask is possible—development groups *can* achieve 10/4 performance levels. Give people the training they need and opportunities to learn by doing, but do not lower your standards or extend the time frames.

As your people learn the process and get good at using it, you will see a change. People will develop an air of self-confidence and a positive, can-do attitude. My information technology (IT) group was recognized with four industry awards in a five-year period. Agile and innovative IT enabled my company to grow revenue by almost 20 percent each year during that time.[3]

REINFORCING FEEDBACK FOR CREATING SOMETHING NEW

In the first step—Define—the project sponsor and the system builder define a goal and the objectives or the performance requirements that need to be achieved to reach that goal. In this step they also create a conceptual design of the business process or the system that will attain the specified performance requirements or objectives (commander's intent and mission orders).

Based on this conceptual design, people move into the next step—Design. In this step the project team expands out the conceptual design to the level of detail necessary to accurately evaluate and implement the proposed new system or business process. Selected technology and procedures are tested for their suitability. Specifications and detailed plans are then created to guide the work of implementation.

In the third step—Build—people focus on executing the implementation tasks as rapidly as possible to deliver the required systems and roll out the new business procedures called for in the Design step. Bigger systems projects are broken down into subsystems so as to implement them within the tight time frames required. As the new subsystems and procedures go into use, they provide immediate improvements and become a base from which to continue working toward the overall business goal. The project team iterates through more Design and Build steps as needed to build out all the subsystems and features needed to accomplish the business mission.

From the perspective of the business executives who sponsor a system development project, the Define-Design-Build process is a way to manage project risk. In the Define phase, small amounts of time and money are spent up front to qualify a business opportunity—5 to 10 percent of the total project cost. If findings warrant, the company then spends only a moderate amount of further time and money in the Design step—15 to 30 percent of the total project cost. In Design, a small, prototype system is created to prove that the opportunity is real and justifies a larger investment. The Build step is where the bulk of the time and money is spent—60 to 80 percent of the project total. The decision to move into Build is made with the greatest amount of information. The nature of the business opportunity and the solution system that will exploit that opportunity are well established.

From the perspective of the system builder, the Define-Design-Build process is a way to navigate through the complexity of creating a new computer system or business operations process. The system builder is truly the person on the hot seat who needs to get things done. The Define-Design-Build process provides a set of strategic guidelines and a tactical framework to structure the work sequence. It lets the system builder set reasonable time limits within which to investigate situations and make decisions in the Define and Design phases. When decisions about system design and budget have been made, this same framework provides a set of tactics for the system builder and the team leaders to employ during the Build phase. The techniques employed in the Design and Build phases give a lot of structure to the work and enable the system builder to effectively lead the effort.

From the perspective of the people on the project team, Define-Design-Build is a clearly defined and manageable repertoire of techniques to work with. People who participate in the project in each of the three phases know which of these techniques they will be expected to use in the conduct of their work so they can focus on mastering these techniques. And there is also an emphasis on working together on tasks in small groups so that the learning and use of techniques among team members is more effective than if they worked alone.[4]

PULLING IT ALL TOGETHER

A business process model can be created that shows how the interaction of the three feedback loops drives a responsive organization. That model incorporates the OODA Loop, the six sigma DMAIC process, and the Define-Design-Build cycle. This model shows that the responsive organization is a network of business units under the guidance of a central unit that is responsible for planning and coordination. This coordinating unit defines objectives (or mission orders) that describe what is to be done and then it assigns responsibility for action to autonomous operating units. These operating units have authority to figure out for themselves how they will achieve their assigned objectives.

The activities of the central coordinating unit (Loop 1—Awareness) are well defined by the four steps in the OODA Loop. The responsive organization is always looking for the mismatches between unfolding circumstances and its own expectations—in other words, the nonstandard input.

The concept of management by exception is nothing new in business, but in the context of the responsive organization, it is absolutely central to the way the organization works. The responsive organization lives in a world of continuous and massive data flows, and it processes this data by using a set of standardized business procedures (in effect, an autonomic nervous system) to handle all routine transactions. The organization devotes its people (its conscious nervous system) to handling only the exceptions and the unexpected.

The operating units use highly automated systems that do not attempt to handle anything out of the norm; they simply focus on efficient processing of the day-in, day-out transactions that drive the business. When anything occurs that does not fit into one of the company's standardized operating procedures (SOPs), then it is picked up and reported to the central coordinator as an exception.

Automated exception reporting systems also notify appropriate people immediately when exceptions occur. Data inputs flagged as exceptions have only one of two possible causes. The first possible cause is that the data or systems handling this data contain errors. The second possible cause is that the data reflect something new that is out of the routine.

In responsive organizations, people analyze exceptions, not computers. If there are errors in the data or in the business operations, people track down root causes and fix them (Loop 2—Balance). If the data is not in error but instead indicates the appearance of something new, then it is very important to have people in the exception-handling loop. This puts them in immediate and intimate contact with the kind of data that indicates a change in market conditions or an emerging threat or opportunity. They can make decisions and act quickly (Loop 3—Agility).

When people in the central coordinating unit of an organization make decisions, appropriate operating units are assigned either to improve an existing operation (Loop 2) or to create something brand new (Loop 3). For actions aimed at improvements in existing operations, the six sigma DMAIC process provides guidelines to follow. When a company decides to create something new, the Define-Design-Build cycle provides the process guidelines to follow. This is illustrated in Figure 5.4.

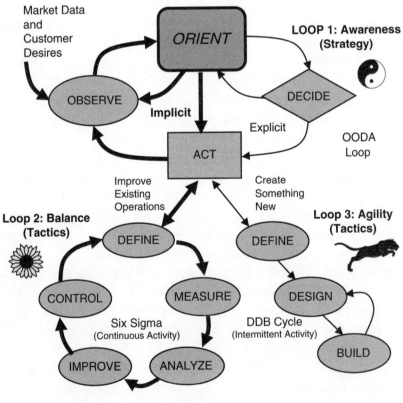

FIGURE 5.4 Process Model of a Responsive Organization

It is important to note that the heavier arrows in this process model indicate the processes that happen most frequently. Responsive organizations usually operate in environments that they already know quite well, and they have well defined goals (commander's intent) that are understood throughout the organization. Implicit guidance and control coordinates the actions of the different business units in an organization. They all have clear performance objectives (mission orders), and most of the time they achieve their objectives through balancing operations that deliver improvements to existing operations as conditions change.

This means a responsive organization has a rhythm to its work and a tempo of activity that is lively but not frantic. It is a tempo that is maintainable over the long haul without burning people out. People in such organizations are not working hard all hours of the day and night. They are not working through weekends or giving up vacations; there is an agreeable work/life balance.

When a new threat or opportunity comes along, some operating units of a responsive organization do go into an explicit agility mode. This does involve activity at a faster pace for some period of time, usually measured in increments of 30, 90, and 180 days. These periods are devoted to creating something new and doing so under deliberately tight time and money constraints so as to stimulate people's creativity and resourcefulness.

These agility projects do call for higher levels of energy, and at times they call for people to work longer hours and sometimes put other activities in their life on temporary hold (like weekends and vacations). But if organizations resort to this kind of activity too often, it will produce burnout and a lack of the very energy and commitment that companies hope to call forth. Much care and consideration needs to be applied to avoid overuse of agility. Most responsiveness is achieved through effective use of balancing, not agility.

A FORMULA TO MEASURE BUSINESS RESPONSIVENESS

If we use the three process loops to describe how a responsive organization works, then we can also create a formula that measures and predicts how responsive a given organization can be. Given the way these three loops work, certain conditions are required in an organization for them to work well, and those conditions can be measured.

I spent an afternoon one day sitting in a coffeehouse in my downtown Chicago neighborhood pondering what it means to be responsive and how to measure the conditions that make responsiveness possible. The place was busy but I got lucky and snagged the cushy armchair next to the plate-glass window in front that looks out on the sidewalk and the grand old apartment building across the street. Watching the other patrons, looking at the people who pass by, and enjoying that burst of mental energy induced by a fine café-au-lait is often a good way to get inspired and be creative.

I started with the definition of responsiveness in business as: the ability to consistently earn alpha profits that are 2 to 4 percent (and sometimes more) higher than the market average. Responsiveness enables companies to earn an additional 2 to 4 percent because they can make 100 small adjustments every day to reduce operating costs and increase revenues. And sometimes responsiveness and agility enables you to earn even more by sensing and moving quickly to capitalize on opportunities for new products or services that, for a while, have terrific profit margins.

I decided to use this results-oriented definition of responsiveness instead of attempting to describe what responsiveness is because we have a lot yet to discover about being responsive; any description I offer now will only change later. Also, I figured that unless responsiveness actually delivers additional profits, why go to all the trouble of being responsive in the first place?

There is one caveat to this definition of responsiveness though; true responsiveness is self-sustaining, not self-consuming. By this I mean companies can always get a short-term boost to profit margins by cutting headcount, reducing customer service, squeezing suppliers for lower prices, and deferring repairs and improvements to infrastructure. But that is self-consuming, like spending down your bank account. It's not responsive because it isn't sustainable; it does not create or renew; it only uses up.

So if business responsiveness is the ability to consistently earn an additional 2 to 4 percent (and sometimes more), then what is the combination of factors that delivers this delightful state of affairs? At this point I ordered another café-au-lait. And as I sipped that hot, foamy, milky coffee, I looked out the plate-glass window and saw a woman walking by with two big dogs; the dogs were so happy to be outside they pulled at their leashes and wanted to charge off down the street. She worked hard to keep them out of trouble.

Then I eavesdropped on a conversation going on at the table next to me. A couple of college students were discussing an upcoming organic chemistry test; one student was showing the other how to read a formula and draw out the molecular structure implied by the formula. Good coffeehouses serve up a stimulating mix of impressions like this to go along with their fine fare, and the resulting blend is often the source of interesting ideas.

Here's the idea that emerged from the blend of that second café-au-lait and the impressions I just described. First of all, I think responsiveness happens when we see something we want and when we are highly motivated to go after it. But we can't just go charging off down the street; we have to focus on what's important and act effectively. Second, I think there's a formula to measure responsiveness, and it goes like this:

Business Responsiveness = (Visibility + Motivation) × Training

What this means is that companies will consistently earn an additional 2 to 4 percent alpha profit if their people can clearly see what's going on in their area of operation and if they have the motivation to respond appropriately. The effect of this visibility and motivation will be multiplied and magnified by the training people get. The better people are trained, the greater the results will be.

This formula identifies the main factors that promote responsiveness and shows how they interact with each other to produce different levels of responsiveness. It points out what factors to measure when we're trying to assess the level of business responsiveness possessed by a company. Visibility can be measured by the technology and procedures a company uses to collect, store, disseminate, and display information. Motivation can be measured by the incentives and authority people are given to make decisions and act to achieve company objectives. Training builds people's skills for using visibility, making good decisions, and acting effectively to achieve objectives. So training can be measured as well.

Now we can start to discuss responsiveness best practices using a common and measurable framework to compare one practice to another. (Did I leave out something important?) This formula is either a very useful insight or the result of too much caffeine.

THOUGHTS ON A FORMULA FOR BUSINESS RESPONSIVENESS

As I think more about this equation, some further details about it emerge that add clarity to what it means and how it can be used in business. Figure 5.5 shows how this equation can help determine the right amount of a company's resources to invest in motivation, visibility, and training in order to maximize the company's potential to earn alpha profits.

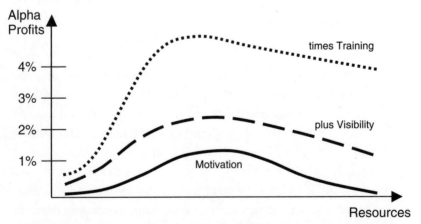

Motivation is the heart of responsiveness. **Visibility** improves the results of motivation. **Training** shows how to put motivation and visibility to best use.

FIGURE 5.5   Business Responsiveness = (Visibility + Motivation) × Training

Visibility strengthens the effects of motivation by providing people with timely and accurate operating and financial data they need to do their jobs and achieve their objectives. They can see if their efforts are working or not and make adjustments as they go. Visibility is also not just making lots of data available to people; that isn't helpful; it just overwhelms them. Visibility means using systems to help people understand what the data means; show them the patterns and trends in the data, and show them probable outcomes indicated by these patterns and trends based on past experience. Then provide people with possible responses that worked well in similar situations.

Visibility is powered by systems that (to some greater or lesser degree) learn from experience and use business rules or decision algorithms to interpret data, identify relevant patterns, and suggest effective responses. Visibility is what enables an organization to Observe and Orient in the OODA Loop.

Motivation is obviously the heart of responsiveness. From personal experience, I believe the motivation for a company or a person to become responsive starts with an urgent desire to achieve some objective fueled by the opportunity to earn rewards for doing so. Then, if there are not enough resources to achieve this objective the traditional way, the company is compelled (feels the fire at its back) to find a "better, faster, cheaper" way, a simpler and more resourceful way. Motivation is what drives people to Decide and Act in the OODA Loop.

You must have some resources; you can't do anything with nothing. But there is a point of diminishing returns; it is possible to have too many resources. Beyond a certain point, you will have so many resources that you are not motivated to be responsive at all because you can do things the conventional way—so why go to all the trouble and risk of doing something new?

If you were to plot out the relationship between motivation and resources on a graph, you would get a bell curve. As resources increase, you see an increase in responsiveness up to some point, and then, as resources continue to increase, you see a decrease in responsiveness until at some point there is no responsiveness at all because there is no need for it.

There is a standard equation for a bell curve graph like this. If we apply that standard equation, then we get this definition of motivation:

$$\text{Motivation} = aR - bR^2$$

where:

> a is a measure of people's desire to achieve a given objective.
>
> R is a measure of the resources applied in a given situation.
>
> b is a measure of the total resources available to a company.

Training is the great multiplier. The more I think about it, the more I believe that just as motivation is the heart of responsiveness, training is the most powerful leverage factor. Since training is often the first budget in a company to get cut and the least often measured productivity enhancer, this would suggest that most companies are missing out on the biggest factor in business responsiveness.

Training enables people to achieve higher levels of performance in all the activities of the three process loops that drive the responsive organization. Where can you get better leverage than that?

SERIOUS GAMES

What do pilots, soldiers, and surgeons have in common? The answer is that they all belong to professions where the cost of making mistakes is very high; and they work in situations where things can change quickly in unexpected ways. They need to be agile to be successful. Training in these professions has become very effective, and the amount of training people get correlates in a positive way to their achievement of desirable outcomes. All three professions have developed similar training techniques to deliver these results. They are currently the biggest users of what are called serious games.

Serious games use simulation and role-playing as ways to teach new skills.[5] Pilots have to log many hours every year in flight simulators, where they learn to handle new aircraft and learn to fly their aircraft out of different simulated emergencies. Soldiers go through countless simulated war games to learn how to deal with situations from urban guerrilla warfare to mobile warfare in open country. Surgeons practice new tools and operating procedures on 3-D virtual reality patients and electronic dummies that respond appropriately when certain actions are performed and when certain mistakes are made.

There is an old saying in training circles that goes "Tell me and I'll forget; show me and I'll remember; involve me and I'll learn." It seems to me that businesses are games. They have a set of rules, a set of operating techniques for getting things done, and the score is calculated by the amount of profits that are generated. In the real-time global economy, companies that adopt the use of serious games are going to be big winners. These days the only sustainable competitive advantage is the ability to learn faster than your competition.

What if companies learned to use serious games to make their training as effective and measurable as the training done by pilots, soldiers, and surgeons? What impact would this have on the ability of companies to truly become strategically focused and tactically responsive?

NOTES

1. John Boyd, as quoted in a presentation titled "A Discourse on Winning and Losing: Core Ideas & Themes of Boyd's Theory of Intellectual Evolution and Growth," delivered by Colonel Dr. Franz Osinga, 20 July 2007 at the 2007 Boyd Conference in The Alfred M. Gray Research Center, Marine Corps Base Quantico, Virginia, p. 55. A copy of this presentation can be downloaded at: http://www.au.af.mil/au/awc/awcgate/boyd/osinga_boyd_ooda_copyright2007.pdf.

2. George Eckes, *Six Sigma for Everyone* (Hoboken, NJ: John Wiley & Sons, 2003), p. 29.

3. This case study was written by the author and first published as an article titled "Move It or Lose" in *CIO* magazine, Vol. 19/No. 9, pp. 32–33, 16 February 2006.

4. The concepts and techniques used in the Define-Design-Build cycle are described in more detail in my book, "Building the Real-Time Enterprise: An Executive Briefing" (Hoboken, NJ: John Wiley & Sons, 2005), see chapter 7 "The Challenge of System Building."

5. An in-depth and informative blog that addresses the topic of serious games is *Future-Making Serious Games* at: http://elianealhadeff.blogspot.com/. Another useful web site on the subject of serious games used in business is *The Serious Games Initiative* at: http://www.seriousgames.org/.

CHAPTER 6

Thriving in a Competitive, Fast-Paced World

"Open your eyes, Pilot. A new world is here."

S o goes the intro to EVE Online,[1] one of a new generation of what are known as massively multiplayer online games (also called MMOGs). In these online games, players from all over the globe log into virtual worlds via the Internet; they learn different roles and skill sets, and come together in self-selecting teams to carry out daring missions in pursuit of common goals. Question: How is this any different from the challenges that await us in the global real-time economy we now inhabit?

If you're part of the generation just starting out in business, answers to this question probably seem pretty obvious. If you're part of a generation that's already been around for a while, answers might not seem so obvious (at first). If you are now in your 20s, you may have a set of skills and behaviors that will become increasingly valuable in business, and you probably developed them through many hours of online gaming. Popular MMOGs such as EVE Online, EverQuest, and World of Warcraft bring together hundreds of thousands of simultaneous online players from countries around the globe to interact in complex, three-dimensional worlds based on themes from science fiction and Dungeons and Dragons fantasy.

MMOGs are not to be confused with single-person shooter games where individual players blast aliens and tough guys, steal cars, and get into street fights. Those games develop fast eye-hand coordination but not much in the way of business skills. And neither are we talking about virtual social worlds such as Second Life.

What we are talking about is online games where there are rules and politics and opportunities to collaborate with others and build your reputation and your fortune. To play these games, players have to interact with each other and build relationships and put together plans and go on missions. They join guilds or corporations that exist in these games; they develop specific skills related to the roles they play (roles like pilot, trader, wizard, warrior, hunter, and priest); and they develop reputations and rating levels based on their successes and failures.

The potential for using MMOGs to develop skills people need to succeed in the global economy is starting to get serious attention. Recently a study titled "Virtual Worlds, Real Leaders"[2] was done by IBM and some professors from Stanford University and MIT. They focused their study in particular on the MMOG named World of Warcraft[3] (known as WoW by gamers) and came up with some interesting insights.

To begin with, here are a few quick facts: They found that currently there are about 73 million online gamers worldwide with a compound annual growth rate of 36.5 percent; the average age of online gamers is 27 years; 56 percent are male and 44 percent are female. Other findings revolve around the concepts of leadership and what we could call responsiveness. Their findings point out the differences in how those concepts are practiced in MMOGs and in the traditional corporate world.

LEADERSHIP IN THE OLD WORLD AND THE NEW

Leadership in the corporate world is restricted to a relatively small group of people who are identified, mentored, and promoted by company senior management. Leadership in the MMOG world is distributed over a wide group of people who work to increase their own skill levels and who are promoted by consensus within the groups they are a part of.

In the corporate world, as the saying goes, it's often not what you know but who you know. In other words, people get a chance for leadership only if they are noticed by senior management. How many subordinates can a senior manager really notice? (And how much dysfunctional brown-nosing behavior is motivated by the urgent desire of subordinates to be noticed?) Since senior management is always only a small number of people, the total number of people in a company who can ever be noticed and get a chance to lead is also small. Lots of qualified people never get a chance.

In MMOGs, players' skills and aptitudes are constantly measured and made transparently clear to everyone; all players can see the skill levels and success rates of all the other players they interact with. Therefore, because everyone can see everyone else's qualifications for leadership, the number of people who can become leaders is large; all qualified people get noticed.

Also, in corporations, once people are promoted into leadership positions, expectations are that those are permanent promotions (unless they get fired). People get promoted because they may have skills that are important at the time of their promotion, but then they stay in those positions even as situations change and the skills that originally got them promoted are no longer relevant. It is hoped that these people can learn new skills, or else the company suffers.

In MMOGs, the expectation is that promotions into leadership positions will be temporary. Players get promoted depending on the needs of the group at a given time for a given situation. As situations change, new people are promoted to lead the group because they possess high levels of the skills called for in those new situations. This way the group gets the benefit of having the most highly qualified people lead them in each situation.

AGILITY AND INNOVATION ARE RELATED TO LEADERSHIP PRACTICES

As I look at what the study says, it seems to me that agility and innovation is the pattern of activity most often exhibited in MMOGs, and rigidity and use of "best practices" is the pattern of activity most often exhibited by corporations. Could this be related to the way leadership occurs in these two areas?

Activity in MMOGs is agile because group members break up their journey toward their overriding goal into many smaller missions that get them where they want to go. These missions require different skill sets so they provide many different players opportunities to exercise leadership.

MMOG leaders are also encouraged to try innovative approaches to solve problems they face because they are clearly rewarded for their successes and not permanently penalized for their failures. And since there are many missions, the risk involved in any one mission is not so great that the failure of one will derail the group's whole journey.

It seems fair to say that rigidity is often the behavior exhibited by corporations because they pursue much larger missions under the guidance of smaller groups of leaders who have fixed sets of skills. Also, since the consequences of failure on these much larger missions are severe, there is a lot less willingness to try innovative approaches. Instead, corporate leaders are often put into a position of trying to avoid blame and cope with risk by following predefined and officially approved best practices (whether those practices are actually effective or not).

If business operations increasingly take place among people who are widely distributed in different locations around the world, and if we live in economic and political environments that are increasingly fast-paced and fiercely competitive, what can we learn from massively multiplayer online games? Do MMOGs offer us glimpses of the way many of us will soon be working?

This analogy might seem a bit overblown at first, but please don't rush to conclusions. I would argue that the main characteristic of online games, the one that enables all the other behaviors to occur, is the real-time visibility and transparency that these games provide. When everybody can see what is going on and everybody can see relevant information about the skills and competency of the people they work with, interesting things start to happen.

Case Study: A Business Application of Visibility and Game Theory

Here's a simple example from my personal experience of using real-time visibility and the peer group dynamic it creates to solve a complex problem. I spent six years as the chief information officer of a large distribution co-operative. Cooperatives are interesting organizations because the members are owners; they are not just branch locations. That means headquarters staff cannot really order the members to do anything; all they can do is negotiate, bargain, and persuade (sort of like politics in a democracy). So how did we get people to coordinate their actions with each other for the good of the entire organization? How did we provide a unified and consistent level of service to our customers?

We achieved this coordination by collecting real-time performance statistics on all of the business units in the network and made this information available to everyone via Web-based dashboards and scorecards. This visibility set in motion a powerful dynamic driven by peer group pressure. Once people in the member companies realized every other member company could see how they were doing, they managed their own performance levels very effectively. No member wanted to be seen as being a poor performer or as endangering our common business by failing to meet performance metrics agreed to in our customer service contracts.

One of the most important metrics that customers watched was a statistic called the perfect order rate. This measures the rate with which a customer's orders are filled correctly, delivered correctly, and invoiced correctly. It's surprisingly hard to nudge this rate above 90 percent and keep it there. And one of the most common reasons for this fact is that

(continued)

errors happen in the translation between the different part numbers used by customers, distributors, and manufacturers for a given product.

This problem was compounded within the cooperative because each of the more than 70 member companies had its own part numbering systems. Each member labeled the tens of thousands of common items that all the members sold with a different part number. And over the years the part numbering scheme of each member company had become embedded in its systems, data files, and minds of its employees. So the idea of changing to use a single unified part numbering scheme was out of the question.

To handle this, we decided that as orders came in from customers, all product numbers would be translated from the customer's part number into a common part numbering scheme called the Electronic Product Code (EPC) (formerly known in the United States as Uniform Product Code, or UPC). Each business unit would then be responsible for maintaining its own translation table that enabled the unit to translate back and forth between the EPC numbers and whatever part numbering scheme it used internally in its company.

We started a project to collect EPC numbers for the products we sold and to help the member companies set up their product number translation tables. We worked on this for more than two years; there were lots of pep rallies and meetings and memos about it. And finally, all the member companies said they were ready to go.

Clearly all the members were not all at the same level. Some had done more work than others, and what we needed to do was set up a balancing feedback loop (Loop 2) that would drive a process where the members quickly got better and better until they all rose to a common high level of accuracy in their part number translations.

In the members-only area of our Web site, we put up a dashboard that calculated every day how many translation errors were occurring with each member company. Member companies got a green star if their correct translation rate was 90 percent or above; they got a yellow sad face if they were 89 to 80 percent correct; and if they were less than 80 percent correct, they got a red, frowning face. We turned this dashboard on and let everybody see how they and the other members were doing. That first week only a handful of members got a green star; some had yellow faces; and many had red frowning faces next to their names. See Figure 6.1 for an example of what this dashboard looked like. (Names shown are not actual names.)

Member Company EPC Compliance Status as of 99/99/99

Member	EPC Compliance	Total Lines	Error Lines	Status
AC Paper Distributors	21%	6,359	5071	😠
Alex Distribution Co.	73%	400	109	😠
Bernard Paper Co.	82%	5,287	977	😣
Camden Distribution	51%	1,986	984	😠
Clarkson Enterprise	73%	3,230	882	😠
Circuit Distributors	0%	3,466	3,466	😠
Darden Paper Co.	84%	19,797	3,173	😣
Dearborn Corp.	81%	8,428	1,648	😣
Dividend Paper Co.	53%	1,944	930	😠
Dupree Enterprises	52%	534	260	😠
Enterprise Paper Co.	92%	19,994	1,756	⭐
Essen Distribution	82%	458	87	😣
Falcon Enterprises	70%	4,182	1,270	😠
Fredrick Paper Dist.	93%	25,349	1,775	⭐
Grady Corporation	56%	2,920	1,312	😠

LEGEND

⭐ = 90–100%

😣 = 80–89%

😠 = 00–79%

FIGURE 6.1 Member Company Compliance Dashboard

My phone rang off the hook for the first few days. Members tried to hammer on me and tell me that their score was wrong because my system wasn't working correctly. I said no, all we did was record every instance where we received an invoice from a member that had incorrect or missing EPC codes. If each product on an invoice had the right EPC code on it, everything was good. If not, even if the same product showed up with the wrong EPC code 100 times, that was 100 mistakes. The measurement was tough, but the good news was, fix a bad product number once and the members' translation rates would improve tremendously. This encouraged members to make especially sure they had good part number translations for their most popular products.

Once the members realized that all other members could see their performance ratings and the only way to improve their scores was to clean up their part number translations, they got busy and fixed their problems fast. That interactive real-time dashboard did more in a very short number of weeks than two years' worth of planning, talking, and pep rallies.

This visibility generated the same group dynamic that motivates players in MMOGs to build their skills and their reputation.

THREE APPLICATIONS WITH GREAT POTENTIAL

There are three application technologies that companies can use in various combinations with each other in order to be very responsive to changing conditions and emerging threats and opportunities. They are:

1. Business process management (also known as business activity monitoring)

2. Business intelligence

3. Simulation modeling

Use of these three technologies can greatly increase the effectiveness of an organization's OODA Loop and DMAIC processes that are critical for its ability to be responsive (see Chapter 4 for a description of the OODA Loop and Chapter 5 for a description of the DMAIC process).

Business process management (BPM) (also known as business activity monitoring, or BAM) is a way for companies to observe productivity in their operations and carry out a continuous, incremental process of improving operational performance. A company starts by mapping out its key processes. The company defines the steps in a process and uses BPM software to collect and display a continuous stream of data that shows the movement of transactions through each step. The BPM software can be used to automate many of the routine tasks, such as moving different kinds of data from one task to another. It can also be set to detect certain error conditions and send automatic alerts to people who need to respond to these conditions quickly.

Business intelligence (BI) systems collect, store, and analyze data. These systems allow people to orient themselves and decide on what actions to take. They collect data from many different sources. Data can be collected from sensors and radio-frequency identification (RFID) devices. Data can be collected by BPM systems or data can be obtained from the many transaction processing systems in a company such as enterprise resource planning (ERP) systems, order entry systems, or customer relationship management (CRM) systems. Once the data is collected, it is stored in a database where people access it as needed.

Often the database is updated with new data on a continuous or "real-time" basis, and summary displays of relevant data are available to people through Web-based dashboards.

When people access the data, they use BI software tools that help them analyze the information and display the results. BI software tools run the gamut from simple spreadsheets and charts to complex multivariable regression analysis and linear programming. The proper mix of BI tools is determined by the needs of the people in a situation and their skill and training levels. The combination of BPM and BI systems is sometimes referred to as enterprise performance management (EPM).

Simulation modeling software is a category of software that is growing rapidly. Because of the fast pace of change in business, companies are faced with the need to make important decisions more often, and these decisions have significant consequences on company operations and profitability. Companies increasingly need to make decisions about how to best operate in conditions they have not encountered before. Simulation modeling has powerful capabilities for improving the quality of decision making in an organization.

Simulation modeling software allows people to create models of things such as a factory or a supply chain network or a vehicle delivery route. Then they can subject the models to different inputs and different situations and observe what happens. A design that may seem good on paper could very well turn out to have problems that are not apparent until the design is modeled and its performance is simulated under a range of different conditions. It is much faster and cheaper to discover problems through simulations than to find out the hard way through real experience.

Manufacturing companies routinely simulate the design of new products and test them out under different simulated conditions so as to get the best product designs before they commit to make them. Airplane designs are tested in simulation to see how they fly before they are ever built; buildings are created as simulation models to see how they look and to test their structural integrity before they are constructed. Why not model and simulate business processes to see how productive they are before we implement them?

PRINCIPLE OF COMBINED ARMS APPLIED TO BUSINESS

Although each of these new technologies is interesting and useful all by itself, their true potential is realized when they are used in conjunction with each other. As discussed in Chapter 4, the military has learned that the most powerful effects from weapons are obtained when combinations of different weapons are used together to address specific situations. By analogy, companies have the opportunity to design extraordinarily responsive operating procedures using combinations of these three technologies in conjunction with their existing installed base of transaction processing systems.

Companies that use BPM systems to manage their work processes can use the BPM process definitions to create process models. Then they can use the data they collect in their BI systems to provide the input for simulating these processes under different business conditions. They can experiment with new ways to organize their work as business conditions evolve.

Existing transaction systems, such as ERP, order management, accounting, inventory management, delivery scheduling, factory control, and maintenance systems, provide a steady stream of data that reflects individual processes in a company or between groups of companies. This data can be monitored through the use of BPM systems to provide a comprehensive end-to-end picture of the productivity and performance levels in these operating processes. BPM systems can update this picture on a real-time or near–real-time basis and show people where the bottlenecks and disruptions are that need their attention.

Once people have identified the bottlenecks and disruptions, they can make use of BI databases and analytical software to investigate the problems and identify their root causes. When root causes are identified, people can design ways to address them. Then, by using simulation systems, they can model potential process changes and see the probable impact of each different change. In this way people quickly select the most effective changes and implement them with a high level of confidence that they will actually deliver the desired results.

A SUPPLY CHAIN GAME

For example, consider a business such as supply chain management or wholesale distribution. Here is a game that has some pretty stringent rules. Players need to figure out how to deliver products where and when they are needed to meet demand while at the same time minimizing inventory levels and holding down transportation and manufacturing costs. If you succeed in keeping down inventory levels and costs but fail to meet product demand, you lose. If you always deliver the products but fail to keep the other factors under control, then your costs get out of hand and you don't make any money.

How does a person learn to excel in this kind of business? In the old days, it was trial and error, making mistakes, and hoping to learn fast enough so that you didn't go out of business before you got good at it. But the learning curve is much steeper now; the rising costs of oil and other commodities are forcing companies around the world to rethink and redesign the supply chains they have built up over the last 25 years. Supply chains will need to continually adjust as prices and other factors change. With profit margins so thin and conditions changing so quickly, it's getting risky to learn by trial and error alone.

What if a company approached this problem by using simulation software to model its supply chain? Suppose the simulation software provided a map and on that map you could locate the factories, warehouses, retail stores, and transportation routes such as roads, railways, and airports that connect those locations. Imagine that you could define the production volumes of the factories, storage capacity of the warehouses, and movement capacity of the different modes of transportation. And finally, suppose you could associate operating costs with each facility and each mode of transportation.

Then imagine you got a real-time flow of data that showed inventory levels on hand at each location and in transit as well as forecasted product demand at each of the retail stores. Now you have a game. The simulation software allows you to try different combinations of factories and warehouses and transportation modes for different products. You can see if that combination will deliver enough products to the retail stores and also see the operating cost associated with each combination.

As demand for products fluctuates, and as operating costs for factories, warehouses, and transportation modes change, you could constantly test out different ways to meet demand while minimizing cost. If inventory planners and supply chain operators could literally draw supply chain configurations on an electronic map display and then run those configurations over some time period, they would quickly learn what combinations produce the best results. They would become immersed and completely involved. People would develop very accurate intuitions about how best to respond to changing business conditions. They would be able to constantly adjust their supply chains to maintain the highest service levels at the lowest costs.

AGILE SYSTEMS FOR RESPONSIVE OPERATIONS

You can't have a responsive organization without the ability to quickly develop new systems as new business needs arise. Business operations and information systems are so tightly intertwined now I'm not sure that there is any meaningful distinction between the two. And since most business operations cannot function without appropriate technology, that makes information technology (IT) agility a requirement for companies to thrive in our global economy.

What is IT agility? I define IT agility as the mixture of art and engineering that delivers robust 80 percent solutions fast enough to capitalize on business opportunities before their profit margins drop. Let's take a look at what this definition means.

First of all, agility means delivering robust systems, not just systems quickly thrown together with poorly written code. Agile systems are stable systems that focus on doing the most important things very reliably. (The concept of *Schwerpunkt* is applied; see Chapter 4.) They are well engineered, carefully constructed, and thoroughly tested.

Agile systems are always 80 percent solutions because they need to be delivered quickly. To do this, they limit scope and focus on addressing only the most important issues in any situation. Systems that try to address all the issues fall into the trap of ever-expanding requirements and endless scope creep, because the other 20 percent is in effect infinite. The other 20 percent is the part that changes all the time. So if you are always trying to come up with a 100 percent solution, do you know what happens? The world simply passes you by.

Agility and the Infernal Dynamic of Scope Creep

In spite of all the best practices and project management techniques, scope creep (and resulting delays and cost overruns) has always been the biggest problem on most development projects. The only way we are going to solve the scope creep problem is to understand and deal with the underlying dynamic that creates the problem in the first place.

This dynamic has two drivers. The first driver arises from the fact that the more we analyze a situation, the more complexity we discover and so the more complexity we add to the design of the system. The second driver arises from the fact that most businesspeople have been through system development projects before, and they know there will never be a Phase 2 on the project (in spite of what anyone says). They know they're only going to get one shot, so they try to think of everything they might ever need and push for all those features to be included in the first phase.

These two drivers set up a self-reinforcing cycle that leads to an infernal, downward spiral of mounting problems. Lots of analysis is done, lots of complexity is discovered, people feel they will need lots of features to deal with all that complexity, and they insist on getting all those features in the first phase. There is a palpable lack of trust between the business and IT people because of this. Inevitably the design requirements call for a system that is way too big and way too complicated; chances of building it on time and on budget are slim to none, and IT is almost always the party that gets the blame.

The answer to this downward spiral is simple yet also counterintuitive. The answer starts by doing less analysis (not more), a *lot* less analysis than is usually thought necessary. Restrict analysis to only what the businesspeople need right now; do not spend time speculating on what they may need a year from now. People know what they need right now because they've already thought about that, and they can usually tell you in 30 minutes or less. It's when you start asking people to speculate about what they'll need one and two years from now that things get complex.

Because you focus *only* on the here and now, you can do less analysis and you can quickly design a system that gives people that handful of useful features they really want right away. And because the design is therefore relatively simple, you can also build the system very quickly and put it into production.

If the first version of the system is delivered in a 30- to 90-day time frame, the businesspeople who need it will be totally surprised (and delighted). They will start using the system right away, and they will thank you for making their lives easier. Yes, they will thank you. They will tell you they didn't think you could get a system delivered so quickly, and they will start to trust you when you say there will be a Phase 2 on the project.

And then, after a few weeks, you start working with the businesspeople on the next round of features they want to add to their system. They will have had time to work with what you just gave them, and they will see what they need next.

Again you are asking them to tell you only what they need right away; they are not being asked to speculate about vague and complex possible future needs.

This agile and iterative system development approach is the way to sidestep the otherwise inevitable scope creep dynamic. Now the businesspeople will stop trying to think of everything they could possibly want and stop trying to cram all those features into one big release of the system. And now IT and business will be able to work together in a more cooperative, trusting, and responsive manner.

A Key Competency for Business Executives

Every well-rounded executive is expected to understand the essentials of finance, operations, marketing, and sales. Now every well-rounded executive also needs to understand the essentials of applying information technology to address common business problems. The rise of the responsive organization makes the use of IT central to a company's survival and success.

Executives can no longer allow themselves to be bewildered by technical discussions (any more than they can be bewildered by financial or marketing or manufacturing discussions). Executives need to apply a basic understanding of how to use IT in business (just as they do with finance, marketing, and manufacturing) so they can make their own assessments of existing and proposed information systems and projects.

There are technical specialists who build and operate computer systems, just as there are accountants who keep a company's books, factory managers who run a company's factories, and salespeople who find customers for a company's products. So executives do not need to know all the details involved in each of these activities. What they need is enough understanding of all of the activities to see how they work together and provide the company with its ability to profitably deliver products and services to its customers.

IT AGILITY ENABLES BUSINESS INNOVATION

In the last several years, a handful of important technologies and methods have emerged to enable the agile IT operations that companies need in order to become responsive. These technologies are not entirely new (nothing ever is, no matter what people may say), but they are significant evolutions and improvements on older technologies.

We will provide a working definition for each of them and then look at a business case study to illustrate how these technologies can be used to deliver agility. The case study shows how to use these technologies in various combinations (combined arms) to enable a company to be very responsive to new business opportunities and at the same time manage its technology risk and operating costs.

Here are some new technologies and methods we'll take a quick look at. A clear high-level understanding of what these things can do and their strengths and weaknesses is essential for the practice of business agility. A working definition for each is presented next.

- *Server virtualization.* Servers are the high-powered little computers that run applications, such as your e-commerce and Web operations or your ERP system and your office productivity applications. We can now connect lots of separate servers together and control them all through a single operating interface. And this operating system lets us provide people with virtual servers (instead of buying new physical servers) by partitioning up the capacity available in a connected group of physical servers and allocating virtual servers to people as they need them to run application systems they are using. This is a very efficient way to operate and optimize the allocation of server resources.

- *Cloud/utility/on-demand computing.* Cloud computing (closely related to utility or on-demand computing) is the packaging of application systems and computing and data storage resources, as a metered service similar to a public utility (such as electricity, water, natural gas, or telephone service). "This system has the advantage of low or no initial cost to acquire . . . instead, computational resources are essentially rented. Customers with very large computations or a sudden peak in demand can also avoid the delays that would result from physically acquiring and assembling a large number of computers."[4] A Web search on the phrase "cloud computing" or "utility computing" will yield many listings for suppliers of this service.

- *Software as a service (SaaS).* SaaS is "a model of software deployment where an application is hosted as a service provided to customers across the Internet. By eliminating the need to install and run the application on the customer's own computer, SaaS alleviates the customer's burden of software maintenance, ongoing operation, and support. Using SaaS also can reduce the up-front expense of software purchases."[5]

- *Services oriented architecture (SOA).* SOA is a method of building new application systems by linking together pieces from existing systems to provide functionality needed in the new system. For instance, a new business application system may need a Web-based product catalog and order entry function, an inventory control function, a billing and finance function, and some functionality to generate various reports. One way to get such a system would be to buy one that has all these features; another way would be to link together these functions from systems your company already has and then deliver them all under a common user interface, such as a Web portal. SOA can provide significant benefits in the form of reduced software purchase costs and reduced time to deploy.

- *Mashups.* "In technology, a mashup is a web application that combines data from more than one source into a single integrated tool; an example is the use of cartographic data from Google Maps to add location information to real-estate data, thereby creating a new and distinct web service that was not originally provided by either source."[6] As with utility computing, SaaS, and SOA, mashups can also be much more cost-effective and timely ways to create certain kinds of applications than the traditional approaches of either purchasing such a system as a package or programming one from scratch.

- *Agile IT system development.* This term refers to a collection of methods for rapidly programming and deploying new systems as needed to support business demands. Several methods are being used. They have somewhat different terminologies, but they all share a set of common practices. The Define-Design-Build cycle is one example of an agile development practice. Those practices include close coordination between business and technical people, rapid system build cycles, and an approach that calls for delivering working subsystems quickly. Agile development iteratively grows a system by successively adding more subsystems or functionality as the business needs arise. System developers skilled in agile techniques make heavy use of the other technologies just listed as part of their ability to deliver working subsystems. (See Chapter 7 for a version of the Define-Design-Build cycle called the 30-Day Blitz.)

Strategic use of systems architecture keeps your core transaction systems running and also enables you to respond quickly to new business situations. The trick is to think of building new business application systems in a quick and iterative manner using cloud computing, SaaS, SOA, mashups, and small chunks of program code. Don't think that programming new applications from scratch or installing a big package are your only options. Companies that master the use of these technologies will set the pace for others to follow.

Case Study: Selling "Designer Chocolates"

This case study is loosely based on a real company that I have observed as a customer for several years, and it illustrates how IT agility makes business agility possible. I have not talked with any of this company's people nor do I know what its actual strategy has been. What I'm presenting here is purely my own ideas of what I would do if I were the chief information officer (CIO) or the chief operating officer (COO) at this company.

This company makes some well-known chocolate candies and sells them through a variety of retail channels. It sells a lot of candy, but profit margins on candy are always being squeezed. I think some smart marketing people in this company spotted a business opportunity to sell "designer chocolates," cookies, and drinks through cozy storefront locations in upscale neighborhoods. The company doesn't sell as much this way as through traditional channels, but it does get a lot better profit margins. It is an opportunity for the company to supplement its traditional business with a new business that can generate alpha profits for some period of time. (No one knows how long though.)

What would you do if you were the CIO or the COO and you were asked how you were going to support this new designer chocolate business? Here's what I would do; here's how I would create an agile IT architecture and leverage it to move quickly and support this new business venture. Imagine that Figure 6.2 is what your existing infrastructure looks like; it was created over the years to support your traditional manufacturing business.

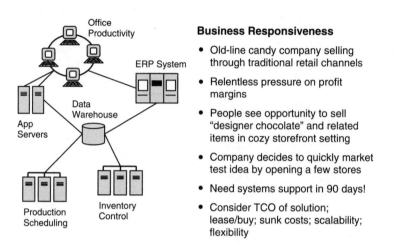

Business Responsiveness

- Old-line candy company selling through traditional retail channels

- Relentless pressure on profit margins

- People see opportunity to sell "designer chocolate" and related items in cozy storefront setting

- Company decides to quickly market test idea by opening a few stores

- Need systems support in 90 days!

- Consider TCO of solution; lease/buy; sunk costs; scalability; flexibility

FIGURE 6.2   Case Study – Existing IT Infrastructure

The key to meeting the company's needs for launching the new business is to leverage existing systems as much as possible so as to hold down costs and speed up delivery times for new systems. What I'd do is use server virtualization to better utilize my existing server base and avoid having to buy any new hardware. Then I'd purchase a very simple bare-bones point-of-sale system for the stores to use for basic store operations.

I'd set up a simple network at each store to connect cash registers and PCs to the Internet. Using that connection and employing agile IT system development methods, I'd use SOA to hook in functionality from the existing inventory control system to manage store inventories, and I'd use the existing ERP system to handle the accounting and financial reporting. I'd create a new supply chain database (data warehouse) to store and report on all the business transactions related to store operations. This would provide the data needed to learn and continually adjust and improve the operating processes of the new business. Figure 6.3 illustrates this approach.

(continued)

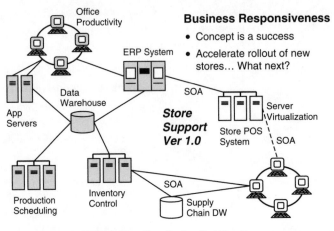

FIGURE 6.3   Case Study—First Iteration

You deliver the first version of the Store Support System needed to open a few stores to test the concept, and guess what? The concept is taking off! Business is good, and now the folks in marketing and sales want to open up more stores and add some new features and products to the business model. Once again you are asked to deliver the systems capabilities needed to make the expansion possible.

How would you use agile IT architecture to keep supporting the growth of this business? Here's what I'd do. I would not buy more servers to support more stores because I'd have to take on the cost and the risk of building out my data center, adding more system backup capability, and hiring more staff. I'd use a cloud or utility computing provider to deliver all the computing power for the stores on a pay as you go basis. This leaves me free to cut back on computing services if the business were to take an unexpected turn and not grow as expected.

I would also combine the needs of the new business with needs of the existing business and look at retiring older IT architecture in favor of using more cloud computing and software as a service to meet changing company needs. This would turn fixed operating costs into variable costs and reduce my need for capital to purchase IT infrastructure. My operating costs would rise somewhat as business grew, but my operating costs would also drop if the business did not grow as expected so cash flow is better protected. The company would not have to incur the risk of a big investment in IT infrastructure at this stage when the business is going through significant changes and long-term needs are hard to see. Figure 6.4 illustrates this approach.

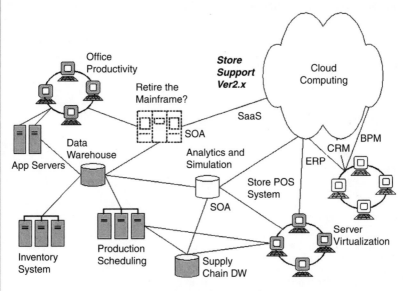

FIGURE 6.4   Case Study— Second Iteration

These diagrams illustrate how a lot of companies are going to evolve their systems architecture in the coming years. Using these techniques and technologies enables companies to move quickly yet also minimize their investment risk in case a new business doesn't pan out.

These approaches are stable and scalable. They enable an organization to move quickly. Ready or not, this is what the future of responsive companies' IT infrastructure looks like.

NOTES

1. EVE Online is a massive multiplayer online role playing game based on a Star Wars type theme; its Web site is http://www.eve-online.com/.
2. A copy of this white paper can be downloaded at IBM's Web site: http://domino. research.ibm.com/comm/www_innovate.nsf/pages/world.gio.gaming.html.
3. The World of Warcraft Web site is http://www.worldofwarcraft.com/index.xml.

4. Wikipedia definition dated July 13, 2008. http://en.wikipedia.org/wiki/Utility_computing.
5. Wikipedia definition dated July 13, 2008. http://en.wikipedia.org/wiki/Software_as_a_Service.
6. Wikipedia definition dated July 11, 2008. http://en.wikipedia.org/wiki/Mashup_%28digital%29.

CHAPTER 7

Ya Gotta Wanna

One of the most important challenges in this global economy is for executives to lead their companies through the process of becoming a responsive organization. As the saying goes, "Ya gotta wanna" or else "Ya ain't gonna." Organizations cannot grudgingly make small changes one at a time and expect to successfully transform themselves. The move from a centrally controlled hierarchy to a responsive real-time organization of autonomous operating units is a significant transformation for any organization to make.

Change is an evolutionary journey; it certainly does not happen all at once. When the process starts, there will be pauses; the pace of change can and must vary, but there can be no stopping. Since change happens anyway (as in we all get older whether we want to or not); the successful company takes the approach of working with change instead of letting a changing world pass it by.

WE ARE CAPABLE OF GREAT THINGS

People in many companies are quite willing to try something new. I see plenty of frustration and boredom when I walk through the "cube farms" of a typical corporate office. I see people sitting in small cubicles looking into computer screens. I see people doing repetitious tasks that often involve reviewing documents to find small errors and then fixing the same small errors and processing the same documents over and over again. This is not work that is challenging or rewarding. It does not exercise the full range of skills that most people possess. This kind of work is stupefying.

In their life outside of work, people raise children, they participate in community organizations, and they have skills and interests that they have developed and grown over many years. They have a lot of talent to bring to bear in their jobs if there was a chance to do so. If people see that their managers are sincere about finding new ways to do things, they will participate in the hope that they can make their jobs more satisfying.

It is also true that the last couple of decades have seen one trendy idea after another sweep through companies. Many of these ideas have been good ones: total quality management, six sigma, lean manufacturing, business process reengineering. Yet employees have reason to be cynical. These ideas were introduced with great fanfare, operated for a while, and then faded away to be replaced by another idea. Nobody likes to be fooled into participating in something that will only dry up and blow away.

Many organizations are ripe for change. Employees are willing, economic pressure is relentless, new ideas are in the air, and the technology exists to implement these ideas. All that is needed is for those in charge to clearly demonstrate that they are committed to change.[1]

Barriers to Change—Why Companies Fail

In my experience, there are two main reasons why attempts at change do not succeed. Both reasons arise from fear (see Figure 7.1). They each create reinforcing feedback loops that cause fear to grow stronger. And

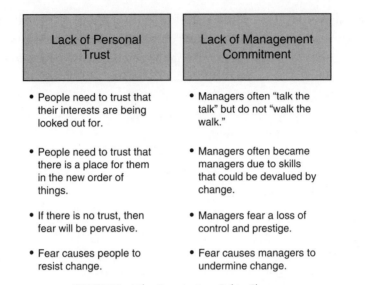

Lack of Personal Trust	Lack of Management Commitment
• People need to trust that their interests are being looked out for.	• Managers often "talk the talk" but do not "walk the walk."
• People need to trust that there is a place for them in the new order of things.	• Managers often became managers due to skills that could be devalued by change.
• If there is no trust, then fear will be pervasive.	• Managers fear a loss of control and prestige.
• Fear causes people to resist change.	• Fear causes managers to undermine change.

FIGURE 7.1   Why Organizations Fail to Change

as fear grows stronger, the organization's ability to change grows weaker until it finally comes to a halt. I have seen this fear and its manifestations cause people to resist change even though it is obvious to all that without change the organization will die. I have seen people win the battle against change only to have the world make them irrelevant (if not completely run them over).

The first reason for failure is a lack of personal trust within organizations. When change is proposed, there is a need to maintain and build the trust of those who will be affected. People wonder what the new way of doing things will mean to their status, to their jobs, and to their incomes. If the information and communication needed to answer those questions is not available or is edited and incomplete, then trust is not possible. In the absence of trust, fear will permeate everything and every move will be resisted.

A basic level of trust between people in a company is indispensable for any chance at effective change. People need to believe that their interests will be looked out for and that there is a place for them in whatever change is happening. If the officers of a company hide information and attempt to fool people into going along with something that will result in their downsizing or outsourcing or simple dismissal, then there will be no enthusiasm and only grudging cooperation from most people.

The absence of trust in many organizations manifests itself in behavior that is the theme of comic strips like Dilbert and TV shows like *The Office*. Many people have gone into defensive mode on the job; they are disillusioned with their employers and feel that the work they do is a meaningless joke. They go through the motions, pretend to care, take on an attitude of indifference, and resign themselves to the notion that there is nothing they can do to change things.

Ironically, employees need to care more than ever about their productivity and the profitability of the companies they work for. No company can afford to keep people on the payroll who cost more than the value they deliver. The global economy with its real-time market forces is constantly setting price levels (and salaries) based on supply and demand. White-collar workers in first world countries will find their jobs increasingly outsourced to lower-wage countries unless they are able to produce more value from their work.

The opportunity is to use the very same technology that makes outsourcing of white-collar jobs so common and employ it to make office and technical jobs more meaningful, more personally satisfying, and more productive. We can give people more control of their time, let them work from home or from a nearby park or coffeehouse; they can reclaim hours spent commuting on crowded highways and days spent in sterile office cubicles. Employees can become much more entrepreneurial and create much more value.

Leading Change Is Management's Responsibility

The second reason for failure to make effective changes is management itself. The employees of a company are no more responsible for the failure to change than the front-line soldier is responsible for the failure to win a battle. In both cases the responsibility for and the causes of failure clearly reside with those in charge.

We have all seen attempts at organizational change where management "talks the talk" but doesn't "walk the walk." What causes managers to do this? I believe in most cases this behavior also is motivated by fear. Managers may intellectually believe that change is necessary, but emotionally there is a feeling of insecurity and uneasiness that effectively prevents anything more than lip service to change.

Many managers became managers because they were good at skills and behaviors that may not be so valuable after an organization changes. Many managers are not sure they can reinvent themselves or learn new skills. They are threatened by people who have the skills and behavior needed to be creative and to be successful at leading change. They fear those people will replace them or somehow render them less powerful.

In many cases the tendency to obstruct change can be most pronounced in the middle ranks of a company. People with titles that range from supervisor to director often have the most to lose in an organizational change. The impact of a proposed change may fall more on them than it does on senior managers. Senior managers can be quite committed to making a change, but it is the middle managers who are in a position either to make it happen on a daily basis or to ignore it or slow it down in 100 small ways.

If a company expects to make the kind of change that is called for to become a truly responsive organization, then its managers, from supervisors to chief executives, need to be committed and confident about doing the work that is required. All levels of management must see advantages for themselves and for their careers in the proposed change. If some managers fear a change for whatever reason, those fears must be identified and addressed. If not, the management of a company will be working against itself, and the message it sends to the rest of the organization is "Management is not really serious; this is just another fad; it too shall pass." This message is summarized in Figure 7.1.

EXECUTIVE BEHAVIOR DEFINES THE WORKPLACE

As much as any single influence, the behavior of senior executives is what sets the tone and level of excellence for what occurs in an organization.

One of the biggest hurdles that senior executives need to overcome is the tendency to micromanage their subordinates. I could never stand being micromanaged myself. As I became an executive, I tried to keep that in mind and not do it to the people who reported to me.

Yet as an executive, under the pressure of running a large strategic infrastructure and systems development initiative, I wound up reverting to bad habits. One day my staff informed me that I was practicing "seagull management," and it was driving them crazy and getting in the way of them doing their work. "What's seagull management?" I asked. They explained it's what happened when I flew in, asked a lot of questions, crapped all over what they were doing, and then flew away again.

There were four separate development projects under way; each had big dollar budgets attached; and I was ultimately responsible for all of them. So I felt quite justified in giving each of these projects a lot of my personal attention. What I learned, though, was that my behavior was counterproductive; the best work happened when I gave people clear directions about what they needed to accomplish and then let them figure out for themselves how to get the job done.

Whenever I'd drop in on a project team and start asking what was going on, it would take them a while before they could describe to me what they were doing and I got the sense they were floundering. So I'd start telling them what I thought they should do. Often I'd drop in like this several times a week. And the more I did it, the more strained things became between me and the teams.

Luckily, I also encouraged and respected people's right to speak up when they had issues and concerns with decisions I made. I encouraged them to offer their own ideas when they saw a better way to get something done. I still do this, and it has saved me more than once.

It doesn't mean people can argue endlessly with me or ignore my decisions, but I want to hear people's good ideas and I want to make sure I don't miss something important and make a dumb move. It can be pretty irritating when someone questions a decision I make; it's even more irritating when they offer ideas that are actually better than my own.

However, I'd rather be successful than egotistical (and I notice the more I cut back my ego, the bigger and bushier it gets anyway—just like a weed). So after several frank discussions with my project teams I began to see what they were talking about. I noticed that people who were actually doing the development work usually had better ideas than I did about how to get things done. All I had to do was give them clear objectives and then let them figure out for themselves how to achieve those objectives. (General Patton knew this before I was even born.)

I came to see that the tension between me and my development teams was mostly caused by the fact that sometimes I wasn't real clear about what I wanted done (or sometimes I didn't know myself) so the teams would start off in a direction that I didn't agree with or didn't understand. Then that triggered me to step in and start micromanaging them.

Here are some lessons I learned from that experience. The first lesson is to be real clear about what I want a team to accomplish. That means a clear description of the system the team is supposed to build and a clear statement of the basic performance requirements, the budget, and the delivery date for the system. Then the team can get to work and fill in the details and figure out how to build such a system in the time frame I give them.

Another lesson is that I need to have a separate project office in place that gives me accurate and constantly updated project plans and status reports. Good developers working on a fast-paced project don't have time to constantly update project plans and budgets. But if I don't get that information on a regular basis, I get nervous and start flying in and asking the team what they are doing. That just disrupts their work, and then the whole seagull management cycle starts up.

Project office analysts work with the development teams to do the work to keep the project plans and budgets up to date. This way the developers stay focused on developing, and the project office staff provide me with the constantly updated plans and budgets I want. Then I can see what's happening. I only get involved when I see something starting to go seriously wrong. Otherwise I leave the teams alone, and they don't have to stop what they are doing to explain things to me.[2]

Good work cannot happen when senior managers practice seagull management. I learned that the more I interfered with the teams and the more I micromanaged their work, the worse things got. After a while they took no ownership or responsibility for their work and simply did as they were told. They did nothing without my approval and waited for me to make all the decisions. Work slowed to a crawl. This kind of management behavior is disruptive and disrespectful. It saps team morale, and in the end it is a self-defeating process that actually causes many of the problems I was trying to avoid.

THOUGHTS ON THE PRACTICE OF AGILITY

The responsive organization is a blend of balance and agility with the awareness to know when each of these two actions is needed. Balance is the action that happens most of the time and involves most of the people in any organization. Yet without agility, balancing alone will not deliver the results a responsive organization needs. Balance enables an organization to continually adjust existing operations and products. Agility enables the creation of entirely new operations and products.

I am fascinated by agility and the conditions needed to call it forth. For me, agility is a combination of creativity and discipline driven by an urgent need to get something done. The practice of agility requires us to put ourselves at the mercy of three masters: the muse, the drill sergeant, and the fire at our backs. This is because these three masters are the ones who teach us the creativity and discipline and provide the sense of urgency we need in order to achieve business agility. You might ask, "Why would rational people put themselves at the mercy of these masters?" That is a good question. And the answer is because there are powerful business benefits to be gained when we learn the lessons taught by these masters.

What follows are several observations and some lessons I have learned in the pursuit of agility.

AGILE IS NOT EASY

Just like the word "athlete," the word "agile" grabs your attention; it sounds great. But going from desire to reality always tests your commitment. I feel good after a vigorous workout, but then the next day (since I don't work out as regularly as I should) I feel sore. And then I don't want to go back to the gym.

Agility makes you sore at first too. But it gets a lot better if you resolve to stick with it; after a while you don't get sore at all—quite the opposite. I see several common issues people have to work through in order to learn agility and get their systems built within tight constraints on time and resources.

The most common issue is the tendency of people to try to fudge, negotiate, or otherwise circumvent the constraints on time and resources that come with agile development.

People want to be agile but they don't like the tight constraints that come with being agile. They offer all sorts of reasons and excuses; they want more time to create quality products; they want more time to do product testing; or they want more time to investigate product performance requirements.

My response is to remind people that the constraints are actually their friend, not their enemy. Accept the constraints and use them to structure the development work; set project scope to make the best use of time available. If people have all the time and all the resources they want, then nobody is going to be agile because there is no urgency and thus no desire.

Another common issue I see is a state of mind epitomized by the statement "That's not the way we do things here." We all (me included) do this. I have no response to this statement other than to ask how the old way of doing things is working out. I inquire if people see some ways procedures could be rearranged or tweaked to better fit evolving conditions or better respond to new opportunities. But if the old way is still good enough (and sometimes it is), then there is absolutely no need to be agile or to change.

A third very common issue that people wrestle with is the tendency to immediately criticize new ideas; we're all prone to it. As soon as someone suggests a new way of doing something, we all think of 10 reasons why that can't be done or why it won't work. Yet, to be agile, it's important to learn to temporarily suspend this behavior, because agility happens when a stream of new ideas starts to flow; when one idea leads to the next and profoundly obvious (but previously unseen) and elegantly simple (yet not simple-minded) solutions start to present themselves to us for our use.

I see project teams experience a rush of energy and insight when this happens, when they make the mental shift from "why we can't" to "how we can." This shift goes right to the heart of the agile mind-set. The high that people get during periods where new ideas flow one after the other is similar to the high athletes get when their adrenaline kicks in and they feel like they can run forever.

THE 30-DAY BLITZ: IT AGILITY IN ACTION

The best way to launch a project is to deliver tangible business value in the first 30 days. I call this the 30-Day Blitz. Use the steps in the Define-Design-Build cycle but shorten them. Do the Define step in 2 days; the Design step in 7 days; and the Build step in 13 days. (Does that sound pretty agile?) There are only 22 working days in a 30-Day Blitz because people do not work on weekends. (Using one weekend toward the end of the blitz is acceptable if needed, but needing more than one weekend just means the project is out of control.)

It's critical to start with fast delivery of something businesspeople can immediately put to use because it provides clear evidence that the project is headed in the right direction and will live up to expectations (at least most of them). People are very busy these days, and they're wary of system development projects because they've seen so many of them fail. They need to see something positive happen quickly before they'll really commit their time and support.

This became clear to me some years ago when I was the engagement leader on a project for a company that provided financial reporting services to firms trading in commodities such as agricultural products, fuel oil, and minerals. This company cleared trades and provided trading data to the accounting departments of the firms that did the trading.

Because it was possible for a firm's traders to do thousands of trades very quickly, the firms felt the need to get better intraday trading data so they could better track the risks their traders were taking. My client decided to invest in a multimillion dollar state-of-the-art system to provide this trading data in a streaming real-time environment.

But, as often happens with such projects, the work got bogged down with expensive and complicated technology that did not work as expected. I was asked to come in and reorganize and reenergize the project. I plunged in and began investigating the project team and the state of the system that had been created so far. I found a lot of demoralized programmers and very skeptical business users.

The project needed the active support and participation of all parties involved if it was going to stand a chance of succeeding, yet people were reluctant to give this commitment for obvious reasons. The project had been under way for a bit more than a year and had so far failed to meet expectations. Who wants to commit to a failing project?

While all the heavy lifting was going on trying to reorganize and turn around this big battleship of a project, I was able to get permission and a little funding for a quick project. It would take some of the pressure off by leveraging existing systems and required just a few weeks of development work to give users some of the most important capabilities they wanted. It would not do everything the big system would do, but it would start providing useful capabilities people could work with until the big system was finished.

This new system is illustrated by Figure 7.2 and it was in production in three weeks. It was built by pulling data from existing systems and combining readily available information technology (IT) components that trading firms already had; the components were office productivity tools like spreadsheets and personal databases. These components were connected together by small chunks of program code to move data and do calculations needed for a core set of trading reports.

The system used a 20-minute batch data transfer cycle to pull data off the mainframe trade clearing system and put it into a trade journal database running on a server connected to the Internet. The data was encrypted using the PGP public domain data encryption algorithm (PGP stands for pretty good privacy, and regardless of it's name, it is one of the strongest data encryption algorithms ever created). A second batch cycle

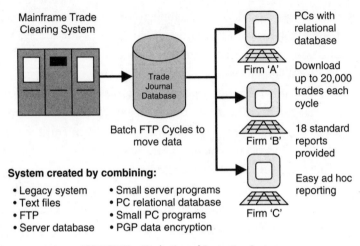

Mainframe Trade
Clearing System

Trade
Journal
Database

Batch FTP Cycles to
move data

Firm 'A'

Firm 'B'

Firm 'C'

PCs with
relational
database

Download
up to 20,000
trades each
cycle

18 standard
reports
provided

Easy ad hoc
reporting

System created by combining:
- Legacy system
- Text files
- FTP
- Server database
- Small server programs
- PC relational database
- Small PC programs
- PGP data encryption

FIGURE 7.2   Trade Journal Reporting System

used FTP to push trading data to PCs in the accounting departments of the trading firms (FTP stands for file transfer protocol, and it is one of the fastest and easiest ways to move large amounts of data over an Internet connection). The frequency of these cycles could be adjusted as needed.

Programs running on the PCs unencrypted the data and updated databases on the PCs. These databases contained some preprogrammed reports, and people already knew how to use the PC database to do ad hoc queries for whatever else they wanted to see.

You may be thinking "Well, gee, that's awfully simple." Yes, it is. That's why it's so powerful. The system went into use fast, and within several weeks we were working on adding the next round of enhancements to it. We were improving the data collection process; we were adding more data security and additional error checking. Users were talking about a whole new set of features to do performance monitoring and alerts.

Here's what I learned: First, people do not care about technology, they just want the needed information and capabilities delivered to them as quickly and simply as possible. Second, keep scope narrow by delivering the 20 percent of capabilities that provide 80 percent of the value. Third, keep IT super simple (KISS); it's often better to build systems where the user interface is composed of common office productivity tools like spreadsheets, Web browsers, word processing, and personal databases. People already know how to use these tools so there is much less of a learning curve.

IT agility like this delivers major business benefits at a fraction of the time and cost incurred if companies go the conventional route of buying and installing large, complex, all-in-one packages. I've applied the 30-Day Blitz many times since. It's a fast, low-risk way to jump-start what can grow to become a very large project. You don't even have to say much about it until you deliver that first big win (so you don't needlessly raise expectations). And once you do deliver that first big win, that robust 80 percent solution, you have the credibility and momentum needed to keep right on going.

AGILITY MEANS SIMPLE THINGS DONE WELL, NOT COMPLEX THINGS DONE FAST

Experience shows me (again and again) that agility is not about working fast but about finding elegantly simple solutions to business problems. You'll know you've found an elegantly simple solution when the businesspeople agree it solves their most important and immediate problems and when the developers know the solution can be built and tested in 30 days or less.

Unless you find a solution that meets these two criteria, it's not possible to be agile. And often, because people can't find these simple solutions, they mistakenly claim that agility itself doesn't work. They come to this conclusion because they attempt to be agile by cramming complex solutions into short development cycles through working harder, longer, and faster.

That attempt has as much chance of success as trying to cram 10 pounds of you-know-what into a 5-pound bag. Inevitably, the bag breaks, and then there is a mess to clean up.

An elegantly simple solution (a robust 80 percent solution) doesn't do everything (there isn't time for that), just the most important things.

Finding this solution is not easy; it's the creative part. It requires businesspeople to figure out what tasks out of all the tasks they perform are the most important ones and what system features they need to handle those tasks. Then developers have to figure out how to build and test a system to deliver those features in the short amount of time available.

Businesspeople need (at least temporarily) to suspend the notion that everything they do is complex and difficult. (They can certainly revive that notion later when talking to the boss about a raise.) A skilled facilitator who walks them through a process-mapping exercise will almost always be able to uncover those most important tasks because in drawing out the sequence of tasks in any workflow, and people's inputs and outputs, it becomes obvious which tasks are the most important.

Then it's the turn of the technical people (at least temporarily) to suspend the notion that everything they do is complex and difficult. After the most important tasks are identified, business and technical people engage in an open give-and-take exploration of features needed for those tasks and how such features might be built in 30 days or less.

Developers can't cling to the idea that they have to write a lot of code to get things done. (This is hard because they often believe their value is based on writing lots of code.) They have to think about ways to leverage existing systems and data and combine components like databases, spreadsheets, and Web browsers with only small chunks of custom code to deliver the features business users want.

This is what the future looks like. Some of the world's largest software companies endorse this idea; many people already instinctively know this to be true.

If system developers insist on writing lots and lots of new code, the project will not be agile. You know things aren't going well when more developers get added to the team, and they start working 12-hour days, and they stop updating the project plan, and nobody really knows what is going on because everybody is so busy. Then they find long days aren't enough so they start working weekends as well; and then they burn out.

Indeed, the developers do churn out thousands of lines of code, but it's just a symptom of their failure to come up with an elegantly simple solution. It isn't possible to write thousands of lines of code and test and debug all that code in the short amount of time available on an agile project.

So, inevitably, when the time is up, and the businesspeople gather around to see their new system, what happens is all that untested code starts crashing during the demo, and the businesspeople are not impressed. What a disappointment.

AGILITY HAS A TEMPO THAT EBBS AND FLOWS

My last observation is about the pacing of agile projects. Agility does require a high energy level, and sometimes it requires longer hours from people. This means agility can only be an intermittent activity; companies cannot expect the same groups of people to perform in an agile manner month after month without appropriate downtime. Do not confuse agility with an attempt to permanently "speed up the assembly line" so as to force people to work harder and faster as a normal state of affairs.

Given that agility has a tempo that ebbs and flows, let's ask the next question: Why would I want to choose an option where I have to think hard, work hard, communicate continuously, stay super organized, and let everyone see what I'm doing while I do it if I also have another option to just repeat clichés, attend meetings, generate reports, and hang out in my office (and various other locations), all the while dealing with the world through deliberately small-bandwidth mediums like e-mail and text messaging?

One method commits me to focus like a laser on getting something done quickly, effectively, and in public. The other doesn't tie me down so much and leaves lots of time open for other activities. One is like committing and then carrying through on a schedule to go to the gym three times a week; the other is like committing to do a study to analyze my weekly calendar and its current time allocations to see if there might be some way to work in some visits to the gym on a schedule to be determined at the conclusion of the study.

There's a saying that goes "Those who cannot command themselves will be commanded by others," or something to that effect. The way

I see it, agility is something I command myself to do because I want to get something done in a timely manner without being excessively supervised or having to take a lot of orders from others. You could say I volunteer myself for this activity because I see it as a way to get something I value: autonomy to do my job as I see fit. I use agility to jump-start a project so as to avoid letting the project get bogged down and lose its chances for success. When I do use agility, I have also learned that all the people working on agile project teams must be volunteers; they "gotta wanna." They must have a burning desire to succeed, and they must reap important benefits when they do.

Agility works best when balanced and mixed with slower-paced process improvement projects. I find people are much more interested in being agile when they know they will have some serious time afterward to slow down. I find the elements that go into making agility happen—creativity, focused mind, high level of interest, upbeat mood, and courage—all have a rhythm; they ebb and they flow.

Agility is a kind of flowing. People do like to flow; yet when they start to flow, they also need the knowledge that when they are done flowing they are going to do some serious ebbing. And if you constrain your agile projects to 30-day iterations, then people know they can handle the agility commitment for that period of time; it's not like they are committing to agility forever. It is not possible to be agile indefinitely.

NOTES

1. An insightful book about creating change in organizations is by John Kotter, titled *Leading Change* (Cambridge, MA: Harvard Business School Press, 1996).
2. Two posts on my blog "Business Agility & Sustainable Prosperity" explain in more detail what I did to set up an effective project office. The first post is titled "Five Questions that Get to the Heart of the Matter," and it presents a clear and concise format to use for project status reports. The second post is titled "Agile Projects Need Real-Time Plans," and it describes the workings of a project office that is tuned to the support needs of agile development projects. My blog is hosted at www.michaelhugos.com.

CHAPTER 8

The Essence of Innovation

R esponsiveness calls for continuous innovation. Responsiveness
means always looking for ways to improve existing operations and
finding simple yet robust ways to respond quickly to new opportunities when they appear. To do this we need to make innovation into a
regular habit, not just an occasional occurrence. It's too bad innovation
doesn't happen from hard work alone; if it did, we'd have all we needed.

But innovation calls for more than just working hard. At the center of
every innovation there is the proverbial "Aha" moment, that moment of
inspiration when you see something about a particular problem that you
had not seen before. I have learned a lot about this moment of inspiration
from my wife, who is an artist. She is a dancer and choreographer, and
I've watched her go through the process of looking for inspiration and
innovation as she creates a new dance composition. Sometimes it seems
to come out of nowhere; sometimes it comes from a piece of music or a
picture; and sometimes, to my surprise, it comes from something I say
or do.

Getting inspiration and then crafting it into a stage production is what a performing artist does. Getting inspiration and crafting it into a business offering (a service or product) is what an innovative executive does. Perhaps no one would call us artists, but in order to foster innovation, we businesspeople need to learn from artists.

HOW TO GET INSPIRED

When seeking innovation we typically ask, "How do we get ideas?" But that's the wrong question. I don't think we get ideas; I think the ideas get us. Artists routinely say their best ideas seem to come from outside of themselves; what they do is give form to those ideas through whatever medium they are working in, be it painting, sculpture, dance, music, film, or literature.

The better question to ask is "How do we put ourselves in a frame of mind where we can receive inspiration when it comes to us?" Artists have been wrestling with this question for millennia. Here are some things I see artists do when they work:

- They immerse themselves in their subjects. Actors immerse themselves in the personalities and histories of their characters, painters do sketch after sketch of an image, and musicians experiment with many different sequences of notes and tempos.

- They collaborate. Many forms of art require effective collaboration between groups of people with complementary skills. My wife works closely with the dancers in her company, lighting designers, costume designers, and musicians. She combines their different ideas to give form to her dance.

- They play with different ideas. They don't dismiss an idea just because it seems strange at first. My wife and her collaborators try out different combinations of movement, light, costumes, and music to see what happens.

Inspiration occurs when a certain combination of ideas suddenly reveals a simple underlying pattern that ties the work together and expresses what the artistic work is about. Artists say they know the inspiration is authentic if they have an intellectual, emotional, and physical response to it. Once that happens, there's a flurry of activity as people flesh out their inspiration and give it shape. During this period, artists work long hours; they become single-minded about bringing their ideas into tangible form and presenting them to the world.

And once a big project is finished or a big show is done, artists leave town. Being creative is emotionally and physically taxing. Artists feel drained after they've done good work. They take time off to recharge.

THE CHALLENGE OF MAKING SOMETHING NEW

Extrapolating from my experience with artists, I see four basic practices that the innovative executive needs to cultivate in order to excel:

1. *Immerse yourself in the business.* It almost goes without saying that you should have a good grasp of the concepts, rules, and systems that guide the business operations of your company. This means a good working understanding of how each business activity fits into the overall business, how the work in each activity is performed, and what the cost and profit factors are.

2. *Collaborate frequently.* Executives need to innovate in the face of high levels of complexity in both business processes and technology. Complexity can be handled more easily if groups of people from information technology and business units work together, bringing their complementary skills to bear on a problem. The innovative executive orchestrates this process.

3. *Tolerate uncertainty.* It is an act of discipline and sometimes of courage to immerse oneself in the details of a problem and resist the temptation to rush to judgment about what should be done. Because of the complexity inherent in most business problems, it is unlikely that the first few ideas to come along will be truly innovative. Don't dismiss ideas just because they defy preconceived notions, and don't give in to pressure to start building something before you get the inspiration you need.

4. *Look for simple patterns.* As you investigate ideas and combine them in different ways to create system designs, look for designs where all the elements fit together in a simple, logical, and complementary fashion. Remember that complex designs for new systems or business operations usually signify that solutions have not been completely explored. When you find a simple combination of workflow processes and technology that satisfy a wide variety of business requirements, only then do you know you have an innovative design.

Simplicity is important to artists because audiences can understand simple patterns of expression more easily, and so these are an effective way to communicate ideas. Simplicity in system and business process design works well for the executive because designs that are uncomplicated are more likely to be built successfully and more likely to perform as expected.

As you and others in your company develop these four skills, you will see a remarkable increase in the innovation that happens in your organization. We executives are already good at working long and hard to get things done. When we combine that ability with an ability to discover inspirational and useful ideas, then we unleash a powerful process for giving our companies the tools they need to compete and succeed.

And remember, innovation is an art more than a science; as you become an innovator, you also become an artist. So do as the artists do when you finish a big project: Get out of town. Have fun. All work and no play makes a dull executive, and no dull executive has a chance as an innovator.

ART, SPORTS, AND BUSINESS ALL BLEND TOGETHER

At the end of a big project a few years ago, I had the opportunity to follow this advice and get out of town myself and recharge. My wife's dance company was invited to be the featured artists at a dance festival held that summer in Prague in the Czech Republic. A hundred years ago Prague, along with Vienna and Budapest, was one of the three great cities of the Austro-Hungarian Empire (an empire many people now hardly know of) and the city is coming once again into a new era of prosperity.

One evening a group of us went to dinner at a restaurant in the Old Town Square, a huge plaza in the heart of the city. The plaza was lined with apartment buildings built in a style called baroque. That means three- and four-story buildings with ornate balconies and red tile roofs; facades painted in pastel pinks, yellows, and greens with ornate trim work framing the windows like oil paintings; and flower boxes full of red geraniums on many balconies and windowsills.

At intervals there were large and imposing church buildings with towering spires that looked out on the plaza. They were made of big limestone blocks darkened and weathered from 700 years of use. The entire plaza was paved in flagstones fitted together and worn smooth from centuries of people's shoes, horses' hooves, and wagon wheels.

There was an enormous TV screen erected at the far end of the plaza to televise the semifinals of the World Cup soccer match: Germany against Italy. A crowd of hundreds gathered to watch. The Germans were waving their yellow, red, and black flags and cheering for their team; the Italians were chanting and waving their own flags. The rest of the crowd was rooting for one of the two contenders; and everybody was whistling and shouting as their favored team made a good play or scored a goal.

After dinner we wandered down quiet streets that led off the plaza. There were more three-, four-, and five-story apartment buildings; these were built about 100 years ago around the turn of the twentieth century in a style called art nouveau. The cornices and trim on the buildings were made into flowing and curving ornate shapes that softened what would otherwise be the straight lines and square corners of the buildings. It made them look almost as if they were each individually hand carved by a different sculptor.

As with the apartment buildings on the Old Town Square, these too were painted in pastel colors with curving balconies and fanciful facades. Some buildings were decorated with statues that seemed to grow right out of the buildings themselves. We walked by one such building with three statues growing out of the columns that framed its entrance; above the entrance was the name "U Tri Musketyru" (At the Three Musketeers). Interspersed among the apartment buildings along the narrow streets in this part of the city were small boutiques and restaurants with Euro modern decor serving wines from around the world and food from many different countries.

We came to a tree-lined avenue where we stopped for coffee and dessert at a restaurant with its doors wide open and tables set out on the sidewalk. I heard French, German, Italian, Slavic, American, and Turkish accents from the diners and groups of people passing by. There were fashionably dressed young ladies talking on their cell phones, office workers in suits and ties walking home, locally made and sleekly designed Skoda cars rolling down the street, and people eating ice cream cones filled with creamy Czech ice cream.

INNOVATION IS A CONSTANT MIXING OF IDEAS

Places like Prague fill me with a sense of how we live in a world connected by nonstop data flows and streaming audio and video transmissions. The spread of broadband Internet connections and the use of information technology (IT; or ICT as it is called in Europe—information and communications technology) is driving our global economy. The spread of information and communications technology, such as wireless Internet, laptops, and mobile phones, enables networks of people to come together to make art, cheer on their teams, and do business. Valuable ideas and inspirations come from the mixing of these activities.

The previous economy, the industrial economy of the last 150 years or so, was powered by networks that largely conformed to national boundaries and language groups. But in the global economy, the networks sprawl across borders and cultures.

Ideas travel a lot faster now and they come from anywhere; no country has a monopoly on good ideas. We are starting to learn from each other in ways that did not happen earlier when nationalism and slower communications got so much in the way. Now the game in business is about recognizing a good idea when you see it, figuring out how to use it in your company or your city, and running with it and extending it even further with some thoughts of your own.

In the agricultural economy, wealth was created from owning land and producing crops. In the industrial economy, wealth was created from owning factories and manufacturing products. In the information economy, wealth is created from picking up good ideas and blending them with other ideas and quickly putting them to use to create something people will pay you for.

The confusing thing about this economy is the pace of change. Unlike the other two economies (which of course still exist; they underpin and make possible the present economy), good ideas and new products now often have only a short shelf life—measured in months, no longer years or decades. So there is a constant urgency to keep moving and keep blending new ideas with the ones you already have. That's a big part of what it means to do business in real time and what it means to be a responsive organization.

Something about colorful and interesting public spaces built on a human scale and full of people going about their daily routines seems central to the stimulation and flow of new ideas. Is there something about these spaces that not only creates but also facilitates the adoption of new ideas?

Are people-oriented public spaces now the places where people (executives, professionals, artists, craftsmen, students) come to get inspired, and discover new ideas, and see how to put old ideas together in new ways? Are these spaces becoming highly productive places (like an efficient factory in the industrial economy or a fertile farm in the agricultural economy) where ideas mix and value is created in the information economy?

New ideas can be hard to accept at first; they can be scary because they push us out of our comfort zone. But sitting in a café on a tree-lined street in a grand old city on a warm summer evening is a friendly and reassuring experience. Places like this help us relax; we look around; we watch what other people are doing. The world seems okay; we smile. Then, in that confident mood and open frame of mind, we find it much easier to let new ideas wash over us, to think them through and see where we could put them to use.

PICTURE OF A RESPONSIVE COMPANY

So, in the spirit of trying out new ideas and keeping an open frame of mind, let's apply the concepts discussed in this book to create a big-picture view of what a responsive organization looks like.

The responsive organization is an amazing innovation in its own right. It is a wealth creation system designed for the realities of the information-based global economy of the twenty-first century. It involves discovering new ideas and combining them with old ideas in new ways. It takes time to think about and accept some of the ideas and operating principles that drive the way a responsive organization works. Responsiveness requires that some very important activities be done differently from what industrial age corporations have been doing for the last 150 years.

We will draw our picture by describing the core principles that define the operating model of a responsive company; then we will fill out the picture by looking at how its senior executives guide the company and how employees of such a company perform their jobs. As companies adopt more and more of these concepts, they transform themselves, and as they do, responsiveness and agility happens. Existing companies can use these concepts to reorganize and revitalize themselves. Start-ups can use them to focus their energy and get best results from their efforts.

Alpha profits generated by responsive organizations will be the basis for much of the middle-class lifestyle in this century, just as hierarchical corporations and the efficiencies generated by the assembly line were the basis for much of the middle-class standard of living in the twentieth century.

FIVE KEY CHARACTERISTICS OF THE RESPONSIVE ORGANIZATION

Five characteristics of a responsive organization create the environment and call forth the motivation in people to become responsive.[1] They manifest themselves in ways that are unique to each organization, but all five must be present to some meaningful degree within an organization for responsiveness to happen. These characteristics are:

1. A transparent and flexible operating model
2. Participatory senior managers
3. Entrepreneurial employees
4. Financial fluency
5. A network organization structure

A Transparent and Flexible Operating Model

If we were to summarize what makes an organization responsive, a good start would be to say that such organizations always employ an operating model with two traits: Everyone in the organization participates in the thinking as well as the doing, and people's behavior is entrepreneurial in nature—they are profit motivated and they seek to constantly improve their performance in order to make more profits.

Responsiveness begins when everyone in a company knows what is happening, when they have reason to care about what is happening, and when they have authority to act so as to continuously improve what is happening. Since everybody needs to think as well as do, access to timely information is critical.

People need to see key performance indicators for the company as a whole, and they need to see in-depth operating statistics for the performance of their particular units. Responsiveness is a real-time game; people have to see if they are on course or off course, and they have to see if their actions are making things better or worse. Unlike the old saying, what they do not know will definitely hurt them.

This full disclosure of ongoing operating results also provides transparency, and transparency breeds trust. Trust is the common bond that holds a responsive organization together. Just as trust and transparency makes the operation of free markets possible, it is also trust and transparency that makes the operation of responsive organizations possible.

Trust is so important because a responsive organization must motivate and facilitate entrepreneurial behavior by all its members. And that happens only when everyone has a stake in the outcome, when programs exist that allow everyone to share directly in the prosperity they generate and also require everyone to sacrifice when the company does poorly. People will buy into such programs only when there is trust and the transparency that gives them the assurance they need to believe they are being fairly treated.

In addition to base salaries, a significant portion of the compensation for all employees in a responsive organization comes from regular bonuses funded by a specified percentage of company earnings (somewhere between 10 and 40 percent of profits). Everybody needs to know what this percentage is; they need to know the cash value of that percentage at any given moment, and they need to know what their share of it is worth.

Because of these bonuses, base salaries in a responsive organization are on the low end of normal. So when a responsive company has a bad year, it does not have to lay people off to lower its fixed operating expenses. It means people can keep their jobs, and they are also highly motivated to figure out how to deliver better profits in the coming year so they can increase their income again. The experience they gain this way becomes a major company asset; it is what makes them more and more effective at working together, and it is how people get better and better at generating profits.

This is grassroots entrepreneurship. It is aimed directly at addressing the opportunity gap and the trap of commoditized jobs that strip work of much of its value. It addresses those things that make employees in many companies cynical about their jobs and distrustful of their senior managers.

The responsive company is organized as a network of autonomous business units each with its own sales and operating staff. Employees in these units are empowered to do anything that is legal and in the best interests of the company unless it is specifically prohibited (as opposed to doing nothing unless it is specifically permitted). This is how authority is decentralized, and this is what enables the speed of action that responsive companies require.

Business units share common services, such as administrative support and financial and marketing services provided by a central coordinating group. In this way, everyone focuses on doing the things that generate profits for them. People in the business units focus on doing things that their customers value and pay them for; and they outsource support activities to other groups that get paid to do those support activities.

IT support is delivered by system builders in each business unit who collaborate with a shared IT services group and with select outside vendors. Business systems are built using technologies and techniques such as service-oriented architecture, software as a service, utility/cloud computing, six sigma process improvement, and agile systems development. In this way systems can evolve in a timely manner to support the constantly evolving operations of a responsive organization. (See the case study example of this at the end of Chapter 6.)

Participatory Senior Managers

Executives in a responsive organization recognize that prosperity is not a function of greed but instead of entrepreneurial employees. They focus on creating and sustaining an atmosphere where this behavior can happen. Senior managers in responsive companies focus on the essentials; they take care of their people; and they *do not* micromanage. They seek out and exploit opportunities to diversify into new markets. They give people clear objectives and performance targets, and they get out of the way. They tell their people *what* to do and let them figure out *how* to do it.

Senior managers actively create the environment for middle managers and employees to succeed. They guide their companies with clearly defined goals and performance targets that are stated not just in financial terms. Entrepreneurial organizations naturally gravitate toward profits, but profits only tell the score; they do not say what should be done to get more profits. So, senior managers define performance targets that also measure customer satisfaction, operating improvements, and product innovation. These performance targets focus on building an organization that can perpetuate itself, not consume itself, and on creating work environments that satisfy people on both a personal level and a financial level.

They build trust by showing and explaining the financial and operating numbers every week; without doctoring or spin. They know that "No-Spin Entrepreneurship" is the only way to build and maintain people's trust in the company and in senior management. Most of the time they practice implicit, not explicit, leadership, leading by example, not by command.

Senior managers also have equity positions in their companies. They put their money where their mouth is; they have personal money at risk. They earn the big rewards because they take the biggest risks. When things go well, they are well rewarded, and when things do not go well, they are not well rewarded. They do not prosper unless their companies and their people prosper.

Entrepreneurial Employees

Most employees do not wish to be the kind of entrepreneur who strikes out all alone to create a new company from scratch; that's more risk than most people want to take. What they desire instead is a chance to work with other motivated people to improve and grow the companies where they already work. They want a chance to learn more about their business and add their own ideas to the mix and make things better.

Entrepreneurial employees recognize that they either make money, bring in business, or support those who do. They know that when the company creates a job, it is an investment that must pay for itself, not an employee right. They will say, "I don't want a penny unless I make money for the company!"

There are no performance reviews done solely by individual supervisors or managers because they are degrading to entrepreneurial employees and are usually mishandled or inaccurate anyway. Instead, employees are continually evaluated by their coworkers and managers based on their experience working together and the success of their entire work group in reaching its performance objectives. Peer group review among entrepreneurial employees provides far more motivation and guidance than individual performance reports ever could. And this peer group dynamic produces behavior that rewards all members of the group, not just selected individuals.

Entrepreneurial employees know that to be promoted, they do not need to show off how smart they are. They do not need to steal credit or attention from their coworkers. Instead, they need to display the attitudes and demonstrate the skills of the new positions they aspire to. Then their coworkers will acknowledge that they are ready to be promoted because it is evident that their promotion will be good for everyone; their promotion will help the unit be more productive and profitable.

Financial Fluency

Everyone in a responsive organization understands the common language of business: finance. They are trained in how to read balance sheets and income statements. Everyone is capable of this because we are all smart people. We can always figure out things that interest us; and since everyone in a responsive organization has real money riding on the business outcome, everyone is interested in the business financials.

In addition to balance sheets and income statements, one of the most important and fundamental concepts of finance in business is the concept of the breakeven point. Everyone needs to know about breakeven points. Everybody in the company needs to be able to do a breakeven analysis on their job or the support activities they perform. This simple calculation tells employees the minimum activity level necessary to pay for themselves and anything else they or the company might do. It allows people to size up situations and determine which ones are worth their time and the company's time to pursue.

Every person in a responsive organization understands how to apply breakeven analysis to their job so that they can do things such as:

- Calculate the sales level at a given gross margin percentage that would be needed to pay for a new investment
- Translate sales levels into relevant business terms, such as the number of billable hours or production levels they need to achieve to fill given sales levels
- Calculate the breakeven level for their work unit given normal billable hours or production levels after subtracting out their variable costs
- Calculate their share of the profits that would result from exceeding their breakeven points
- Know how much money they would lose if they do not reach their breakeven points

People at each level of a responsive company know their operating numbers and their breakeven points better than senior management does. Because of this, activity levels necessary for higher profits become clear to everyone; people see what their share of the profits (or the losses) would be. This common understanding is extremely powerful; it is the foundation for the effective entrepreneurial behavior that responsive organizations depend on.

A Network Organization Structure

The organization structure of a responsive company does not look much like the traditional pyramid-shape hierarchy of a twentieth-century industrial corporation. It looks more like a swarm, a school of fish, a flight of birds. The business units are connected and all moving in the same direction, but they are each thinking and acting for themselves. Units can act on their own as opportunities arise. And if an opportunity proves to be a big one, then the company creates new business units to grow into those new markets. This network organization structure promotes swarming behavior and is illustrated in Figure 8.1.

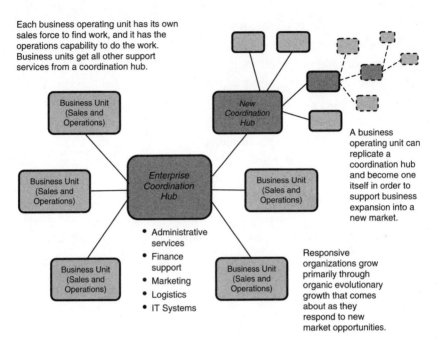

Each business operating unit has its own sales force to find work, and it has the operations capability to do the work. Business units get all other support services from a coordination hub.

A business operating unit can replicate a coordination hub and become one itself in order to support business expansion into a new market.

Responsive organizations grow primarily through organic evolutionary growth that comes about as they respond to new market opportunities.

FIGURE 8.1   Structure of the Responsive Organization

In every responsive organization there are ongoing conversations about where to centralize certain functions to get economies of scale and where to forgo economies of scale in order to get more autonomy and responsiveness from the business units. But at no time does the notion of centrally controlled economies of scale ever become the main business strategy or the dominant operating policy.

SUSTAINABLE PROSPERITY

Responsive organizations always focus on building and harnessing the entrepreneurial energy of their members; that is the main driver of their business strategies. They understand that in the competitive and unpredictable world we live in, responsiveness driven by the entrepreneurial energy of autonomous business units is a more profitable course to follow than the course of centrally controlled operations and economies of scale.

The whole world has become like a stock market; events unfold in bewildering and unpredictable ways. The responsive organization embraces this state of affairs and learns to use it to its advantage. Responsive organizations generate alpha profits because of their ability to make many small adjustments every day to improve their performance as conditions change and because of their ability to move quickly to seize new opportunities as they come along.

If change is the one predictable thing in a world where so much else is so unpredictable, then companies optimized to deal with change will certainly be more successful than companies not optimized to deal with change. That is why responsiveness trumps efficiency; that is why responsiveness and the business practices that bring it about are the basis for sustainable prosperity in this century.

NOTE

1. These five key characteristics come from summarizing my personal observations and also from a series of conversations over the last several years with a successful entrepreneur and business executive named Michael Chakos. Mr. Chakos is currently president of a mid-sized industrial services company named North American Coatings, LLC (http://www.nacoatings.com/). Over the last 10 years he has employed these five characteristics in his company and found them to be very effective. His insights have helped to shape and refine my own ideas.

A

Executive Checklist for Monitoring Development Projects

Here's a crash course for business executives in what they need to know to sponsor information technology (IT) system development projects. Business executives who sponsor system development projects need a way to assess them as they move through the Define, Design, and Build sequence. These questions and the answers provided can be used to assess any IT development project, and they will reveal quite clearly whether things are going well.[1]

The questions listed here will enable an executive to assess development projects from three perspectives that cover all the important aspects of system development. Those three perspectives are:

1. Goodness of system design

2. Progress made developing the system

3. Competence and confidence of people on the project

1. GOODNESS OF SYSTEM DESIGN

In the first two to six weeks of the project—the Define phase—ask yourself and the system builder in charge of the project these questions:

1. *What is the business goal of the project?* In two sentences or less, state the action the company is going to take and the desired result of that action. This is the goal. It is the target, the destination the project is supposed to reach. Figure out what it is, or stop the project.

2. *Which performance criteria is the system supposed to meet?* State requirements that the system will meet in these areas:[2]
   a. Business operations
   b. Customer expectations
   c. Financial performance
   d. Company learning and improvement

   These are the specific measures that will determine whether the system will be a success. Make sure that you and the people designing and building the system know what they are.

3. *Do you believe that a system that meets the preceding performance requirements will accomplish the business goal you are striving for?* If you have a feeling that important performance requirements have been left out, add them before the project gets any further along, but make sure that you add only requirements that are strictly necessary to accomplish the business goal. Requirements that are too broad will result in increased system complexity and less chance that the system can be built successfully.

4. *Which existing computer systems in your company does the new system design leverage?* The new system should leverage the strengths of systems and procedures already in place. That way it can focus on delivering new capabilities instead of just replacing something that already exists. If you decide to replace everything and build from a clean slate, you had better be prepared for the considerable extra time and expense involved and be sure that it's worth it.

5. *Does the overall design for the new system break down into a set of self-contained subsystems that can each operate on its own and provide value?* Large computer systems are really made up of a bunch of smaller subsystems. Your company should be able to build each subsystem independently of the others. That way, if one subsystem runs into problems, work on the others can still proceed. As subsystems are completed, they should be put into production as soon as possible to begin paying back the expense of building them. If all subsystems must be complete before any can be put to use, that's a very risky, all-or-nothing system design. Change it.

6. *How accurate is the cost-benefit analysis for the new system?* Have the business benefits been overstated? Would the project still be worth doing if the business benefits were only half of those predicted? Cost-benefit calculations usually understate costs and overstate benefits. You are the one who is best able to judge the validity of the calculations. Do you believe they are accurate? The bigger and riskier the project, the greater the benefits must be to justify the risks and expense. Don't spend more on a system than it's worth.

7. *How has the system builder demonstrated that his or her system design and project leadership skills are appropriate to the demands of the project?* If you don't have a qualified system builder in charge, the project will fail from lack of direction. Management by committee won't work. If this person lacks the necessary design and leadership skills, he or she must be replaced, no matter what other skills the person may possess.

8. *Which of the strategic guidelines have been followed, and which have not?* If you follow all seven of the strategic guidelines (see Appendix B), the design of the system is very good. It's acceptable if one of the guidelines—except the first one—isn't followed. If two aren't followed, there had better be very good reasons. In that case, determine which extra precautions will be taken to compensate for the increased risk. If more than two of the guidelines aren't followed, the design is fatally flawed. The system can't be built on time or on budget, if it can be built at all.

9. Each significant system feature should be described in a manner that provides meaning and value to your organization. Each system feature should have a statement behind it that follows this pattern: As X (X is a role such as salesman for instance), I need system feature Y (Y is a feature such as a calendaring feature) so that I can achieve business benefit Z (Z is a benefit such as timely follow ups and should have a dollar value attached to it).

2. PROGRESS MADE DEVELOPING THE SYSTEM

As the project moves through the design and build phases, ask yourself, the system builder, and the project teams these questions:

1. *Are the project plan and budget in place? Do people pay attention to the plan?* Is there a project office group that provides regular and accurate updates to the plan and the budget? Multimillion-dollar system development projects involve a lot of people and stretch across some period of time. The project plan is the central co-ordinating instrument that tells every person exactly what he or she is supposed to be doing at any given time. If the plan isn't kept current, the people on the project have no way to coordinate their work effectively. The system builder will lose track of the details. Delays, cost overruns, and confusion will result. People won't know how much has been spent to date or how much more is required to finish. When this happens, the project goes into a death spiral.

2. *Are the subsystem teams organizing their work into clearly defined design and build phases?* Are these phases getting done on time and on budget? The project team working on each subsystem should spend one to three months creating a detailed design and system prototype (Design phase). The detailed design should then be turned into a working system within two to six months (Build phase). If things take longer than this, the project is moving too slowly and it will lose momentum and drift. It's the system builder's responsibility to keep things organized and moving. Make sure this person is capable.

3. *What's the situation this week?* Spot-check the project plan and budget from time to time. Have the system builder review the current project plan with you, show you the money spent to date on each subsystem, and the estimate for remaining time and budget to complete each subsystem. Do you believe what you hear? Can the system builder explain the situation clearly, without tech talk? How does the most recent estimate of time and budget compare to original estimates? Is it still worth the cost to complete the project?

4. Each week (or even each day) the system components developed to date should be assembled and tested to demonstrate that they work together as expected. This will avoid costly system integration issues later on and it proves that the system will operate as designed.

3. COMPETENCE AND CONFIDENCE OF PEOPLE ON THE PROJECT

Ask these questions of yourself, the system builder, and the project teams:

1. *What are the design specifications?* As each project team completes its Design phase, ask them to show you the acceptance tests, the domain model, the process flow diagrams, the logical data model, the user interface and the technical architecture for their subsystem. Can they tell you how this system will deliver the business benefits in the cost-benefit analysis? Do the design specifications make any sense? Do the people on the team know what they're talking about?

2. *Are the project team members as confident as the project team leaders? Are the team leaders as confident as the system builder?* If people believe they have the right skills and a good system design, they will be confident in their ability to build the system. If people at every level don't share and reflect this confidence, there's a problem somewhere. If people are trying to transfer onto the project, that demonstrates confidence. If people are transferring off the project or leaving the company, that indicates lack of confidence. Expect the project to fail.

NOTES

1. All of these questions are explained in greater detail in my book *Building the Real-Time Enterprise: An Executive Briefing* (Hoboken, NJ: John Wiley & Sons, 2005).
2. These four perspectives that create a comprehensive view of an organization's performance are defined by Robert Kaplan and David Norton in their book *The Balanced Scorecard: Translating Strategy into Action* (Cambridge, MA: Harvard Business School Press, 1996).

B

Seven Strategic Guidelines for Designing Systems

1. *Closely align projects with business goals.* No system development project can be successful until you have first identified the business opportunity that makes the system worth building. And no system will benefit a company unless it supports the effective exploitation of the opportunity it was built to address.

2. *Use the system to change the competitive landscape.* Look for opportunities to create a transformation or value shift in your market. Find ways to provide big cost savings, significant productivity increases, or whole new product features that will surprise and delight your customers.

3. *Leverage the strengths of existing systems.* Build new systems on the strengths of older systems. When existing systems have been stable and useful over time, find ways to incorporate them or parts of them into the design of new systems.

4. *Use the simplest combination of technology and business procedures to achieve as many objectives as possible.* A simple mix of technology and business processes that can achieve several different objectives increases the probability that at least some of these objectives will be achieved. This simple mix reduces the complexity and risk associated with the work and spreads the cost across multiple objectives.

5. *Structure the design to provide flexibility in the development sequence used to create the system.* Break the system design into separate components or objectives, and, whenever possible, run the work on individual objectives in parallel. In this way, delays in the work toward one objective will not impact the progress toward other objectives.

6. *Don't try to build a system whose complexity exceeds the organization's capabilities.* When defining company goals and the systems needed to accomplish those goals, aim for things that are within reach. Set challenging but not hopeless goals.

7. *Don't renew a project using the same organizational approach or system design after it has already failed.* Redoubled effort and hard work are an inadequate response for ensuring the success of a project after in has once failed. The new approach must clearly reflect what was learned from the previous failure and offer a better way to succeed.[1]

NOTE

1. Sir Basil Henry Liddell Hart, *Strategy* (New York: Penguin Books, 1967). I came across Liddell Hart's book years ago and found Chapter 20, "The Concentrated Essence of Strategy" to be one of the most lucid and succinct discussions of strategy I have ever read. My seven strategic guidelines for designing systems are much influenced by his book.

Index